Wind

A Novel of the Ice Age

PATRICIA KRANISH

ISBN 978-1-54398-479-8 (print)

ISBN 978-1-54398-480-4 (eBook)

PRAYER FOR A CHILD BORN IN WINTER

Mother, wait a little longer.
My child is hungry and cries for me.
The sea that held her
Satisfies the earth for now.

INTRODUCTION

Twenty-five thousand years ago, small, migrating bands of hunters and foragers traced converging paths across the freezing earth. Evidence of their existence is etched in their long-buried bones, turned to stone as hard as the tools they shaped over the millennia. They followed the vast herds that flourished as the earth cooled and the seas lowered, adapting to hard life in arctic and desert, forest and savannah.

They traveled immense distances to trade objects—some vital, some merely useful, others prized for beauty alone. What knowledge and beliefs did they also exchange, what features and bloodlines? Did they have a religious ideal or a moral code? Were they altruistic, practicing a selfless tribalism for the greater good, or were they governed by base instinct that allowed only the strong and ruthless to survive?

Proof of their humanity, along with suggestions of cruelty, have endured: a splinter of bone that required the tender help of another person to heal; a shard of rib cage shattered by a spear. Teeth worn flat like overused tools freed nimble hands to create artifacts of lasting grace, utility, and imagination.

They were predators and prey. They made up for what they lacked and what they feared by shaping the equivalent of tooth and claw, weight and warmth. They took only what they could carry on their backs, staying in one place just long enough to strip the fruit from their knotty stems.

They competed with the birds for the berries, swallowing flinty seeds, bitter leaves, and unyielding rind, their hard stomachs wringing the last bit of nutrition to sustain their strength. When the final fruit was plucked, and their prey took flight, they moved on in a race against time, when the ground would freeze and the vines would fold into the harsh sleep of winter.

The Huul is part of the Fertile Crescent and extends to the Mediterranean Sea in the West. The clans of the Huul, the Nir, Willow, NesGras, and Wolf Moon, meet yearly for marriage, trade, sport, and companionship—weather and current alliances permitting.

CHAPTER ONE

NEW LIFE

Look closely at the mountain that rises across the valley. What first appears to be ascending columns of goats are people: three men, three women, and three children. Two of the women carry infants in woven slings tied across their chests. You see them, but they cannot see you across the expanse of years. The eternal, blue-green sea that bounds their world on the west is black in the waning light and licks the base of the mountains. Since then, of course, the weather has warmed and dried before the retreating ice. Their ancient path is slippery with snow, and frost collects along the ledges and crags in anticipation of an Ice Age winter.

See how sure-footed they are, how they support each other. While there are rough bushes and yellow grasses on your side of the divide, they climb among abundant evergreens, an alpine setting of glacial ponds and meadows. It is not winter, yet the wind that pushes against them blows from the frigid north. Their hair and outer garments fly out behind them, stiffened and blanched by frequent rain. They bend toward the mountain, hunched against the force that is intent on breaking their stride. The wind is the enemy that they fight and fear. They call themselves the NesGras, and they are people of the Huul, the crescent of land that curves around the vast, enduring sea.

They have secret names we will never know. The tallest and oldest of the men we call Esur. He bows under the weight of hides and poles that they use for shelter. He struggles to keep his pregnant wife from falling on the skittering rocks and icy puddles. She is called Mother and her name will be buried with her.

Esur presses his arm, stiff and sinew swollen, against the small of her back and grips her garment with his fingers to steady her. At her other side, her sister Mina wears her baby carrier tied tightly around her body, her newborn son snuggled safely against her heart. Mina strokes her sister and whispers to her, "Just a little while longer, and we will rest."

The children stay close behind. Xur is seven years old and his sister Sura is two winters younger. Their cheeks tremble with the effort to keep from crying. Only this morning, Mother's legs were agile and quick like all people who make the mountains their home. She plaited their dark hair and rubbed their round faces with oil and sang a nonsense song with them. The children laughed at the absurd sounds they made until an abrupt pain silenced her singing and they cried out for help. The others came running, pulling on clothing, dropping what they gathered, and picked up their tools and moved without wasting motion or time. They were a steep climb away from their hollow shelter and they had to reach it before dark. "Wait, Mother, wait," they said, as if to hold the darkness at bay until they could reach the sheltered higher ground.

"We are here, Esur," Rosh said to his brother. He lit a torch and entered a high-ceilinged cave. The odor of chalk and the droppings of vacated bats bled into the air and stung their throats and eyes. Esur rolled his burden of tools on to the ground while supporting Mother with his right arm. Mina swept the floor clear of tiny mouse skeletons suspended in the detritus of the animals that had overrun the cave in their absence. Mina set their pallets, layers of straw and hides, in a circle and ignited a fire in the center of the circle. She laid her newborn son, Nin, on the bedding nearest the spreading warmth. Rosh's wife placed her own infant daughter next to him. Her oldest girl, born a year before Sura, watched the women. As they prepared the cave for birth, the cold and dreary hollow in the veins of the mountain dissolved into a living, pulsing organism.

"Too soon." Mother's voice scratched the air. The pain that started earlier in the day quickened, sharp as a spike through her spine. It ebbed and flowed, each wave more brutal than the last. She tried to bend her knees and raise herself to a crouch and fell back on the pallet, amazed at the brutal force that kept her down.

The flames burned the dampness out of the air and lit the dark corners. Mina rendered the marrow of a goat. Rosh's wife made a poultice of willow bark and massaged Mother's hard and unyielding belly. Mother heaved and contracted, yet the mound shaped by the unborn child remained high and undescended. Her voice ground out without words, like wind forcing its way between cracks in the cave wall. For moments at a time she would fall into an immobile sleep, then the pain would provoke her. She cried for water, for her mother, for her children. She appealed to her reluctant child, to the living wind, and to the fire that consumed her from the inside. Mother's hands that had lovingly received the newborn Nin from Mina's body only weeks before now tore at her own garments as if the cloth were a rabid animal assaulting her flesh. Sura had watched her mother cradle the top of Nin's emerging head, and he seemed to glide all at once from being a part of his mother to being a small and noisy presence of his own. Now Mother twisted and writhed as if the wind itself had entered her and cleaved her in two. All three women of this NesGras clan became pregnant toward the end of the last winter. The two children born so far, Mina's robust son and the tiny girl called Hyssop, surprised them with joy and hopefulness. Each child was a strand in the rope that fortified the life of the clan. Each child's death ruptured the continuity of its existence. Fear hovered beyond the hearth, waiting in the darkness.

Outside, a driving rain beat the wilted leaves of an oak tree. Esur silently beseeched the spirits of wood and fire, of water and stone, to spare this woman and her child of the wind. Esur, who saw life as a path to be walked until one could walk no more, wanted suddenly to be able to rest, to offer comfort to his wife as she comforted him when his body and spirit ached. He repeated her name. He would rather that a limb be torn from his body than to walk this path without her.

Esur helped block the entrance to the cave. Xur, his ears tuned to his mother's cries like a wary fawn, dragged branches as big as himself to the opening. Xur was born big and strong—almost ready to walk they said—howling with hunger and life. Mother laughed when she examined him. "He looks like you, Esur, but already he makes more noise." Since the birth of Sura, two more children were born weak and withered and soon died. They placed the small bodies in the earth, first one, then another, and waited for their restoration. *Nothing is lost*, they prayed, then they moved on. Over time, the fruitless labor sapped Mother's body and spirit, and her smile became a taut line across her face. How could her children know what she kept inside? She hid the red effusion that poured from her body and buried it in the dust. Her own mother died when her sister Mina was born, and the unstoppered bleeding colored her dreams ever since.

The keen of the women echoed the whir of the branches in the wind. Esur was afraid to turn or even listen. Was it life or death that clamored at his back? Was it Mother's cry of loss or a filling of lungs with first breath?

"Esur, the boy is alive," said Mina, coming up behind him. He reentered the cave, not looking at Sura, who cradled a small, whimpering bundle. He passed the others who looked at him from under lowered brows. Mother turned her eyes toward his face as Esur knelt beside her and reached for her hand. His heart clenched—her face, her shoulder, all along one side of her body was cold and rigid, as if half of her was already dead. Mother's breath rattled like dry seeds. She strained to take hold of Esur's hand. They touched, hand folding into hand, as if willing life through their fingertips. Mother, her last strength gone, exhaled her spirit with her final breath and was still.

Esur, who never showed fear or anger, who spoke the words of his father to his children as his duty commanded, who would have been content to live alone in silence before he met Mother, bellowed his grief in a cry that echoed through the cave. The desolation resounded against the stony walls, and one by one, the others began to weep, not for this one death alone, but for all the dead who had gone before, and for all the deaths to come, and for the cruelty of life in between. It was not their way to speak of weakness or to question the circumstances of their existence. The Spirits, whom they invoked and propitiated for help, could not control their own impulses much less ease the way for man. They called upon them nonetheless.

The new infant flexed his thin arms and legs, his tiny fingers and toes. His eyes snapped open and seemed to search Sura's face. Black hair, soft and plentiful, started at the crown of his head. Even his tiny face was covered with fuzz. Sura gently opened the wrap that swaddled him and turned him over. The fine hair grew down his back and ended in a little swirl at the base of his spine, hair that would mostly fall, should he survive. His behind, smaller than Sura's fist, was still blue, and his little stick legs drew up tightly across his body. The umbilical cord tied off with twine still pulsed with his mother's blood. He began to cry. His cries were piercing and insistent, and drowned out the tears of all the others in the cave except Esur. Death is passive and silent; new life is demanding and cannot be ignored. So Sura wrapped him once again in his deerskin coverlet. His eyes brimmed with a newborn's unshed tears as he put two middle fingers of his hand into his mouth and sucked. Sura, her child's heart sore with loss, whispered to her tiny brother, "You are Bani. Stay with us then." And all within the cave prayed that he would.

Esur held Mother until the women began to gently cleanse her body. Mina gathered drops of liquid from Mother's breast on her fingers and fed them to the infant so he would remember something of his mother. She gently folded her sister's arms and legs across her body, bending her limbs at the joints into the posture of a sleeping newborn. She wrapped the body slowly in unworn doeskin clothes just as a newborn is swaddled at birth. Mother would be buried in the morning in a high cave, a NesGras vault for their dead, her feet unbound, free to take her spirit back to her mother's campsite. On her left ankle was the scarified mark of the Willow, the clan to which she was born, and above that, the mark of the NesGras, the clan to which she belonged through her bond with Esur. The scars were rubbed with the red ochre of the mountains of the Huul so that even in eternity, her place would be recognized.

CHAPTER TWO

THE DEER

Sura, newly blood initiated into the dwindling society of NesGras women, woke last. Hyssop, bow-legged and slight for her eight years, hovered over her, and before Sura's eyes could focus on her, Hyssop lisped through a gap in her new front teeth, "Braid my hair." Sura frowned at her. "If you will," the child added and smiled, forgiven as usual for her small breach of courtesy.

The embers from the night's fire still glowed. Smoke drifted up toward an uneven opening high above the floor and was expelled like warm breath, heavy and visible in the cold. A child coughed in his sleep then turned over on his side and was quiet. Mina stretched and shivered like a cat waking in the sun. She reached for her blanket and wrapped it around her. She moved the interlaced branches that obscured the entrance of the cave and gathered an armful of firewood left outside the day before. A rush of frigid air routed the nestling sleepers as the dawn rolled over the hills and chased the darkness.

Sura watched Mina build the fire one branch at a time. Crushed and bitter grains simmered and popped over heated rocks. They turned a gold-flecked brown and sweetened the air. She sat up and looked at the little girl. Hyssop was golden and brown, too. The low fire framed her in light, and her eyes were the bright dark of polished pecans. "Come here," Sura said, reaching for her and wriggling her fingers. "You look delicious."

Hyssop giggled as Sura settled her on her lap and ruffled her sleep-flattened hair. The skin on her knobby little arms and legs was as soft as the velvet of antlers. While the other children were shooed away, encouraged to run and explore, Hyssop was embraced and kept close. She was not the youngest, just small enough to be set on someone's shoulders and carried. *Little Bones* her mother called her and picked her up when she fell, shielding her fragile frame against the edges of rocks and ground and ice. Even Esur patted her head with a gentle touch—something Sura could not remember him doing to her, or to anyone else either.

"Tell me about the day I was born, Sura. About the hyssop blooming in the rain."

"I told you that yesterday. You tell me a story."

Hyssop took a deep breath and began: "One day, when I was a baby, I disappeared. My mother looked everywhere. 'Where is my little flower?' She cried so much." Hyssop spread her arms as wide as she could. "Everyone searched their clothes, and shook out the blankets. She overturned every pot. She moved every stone. Did an eagle think I was a mouse and take me to the sky?" Hyssop paused dramatically, bent closer to Sura, and whispered, "That could have happened you know."

"Did they ever find you?" asked Sura, pulling a twig comb through the child's tangled curls.

"Yes," said Hyssop, "I was so small that an oak leaf fell and covered me all up."

Sura laughed. "Mother did find you under a pile of leaves."

Hyssop's own mother, Zu, had fallen asleep with the infant beside her. When she woke up, the tiny girl wasn't there. It was Mother who brushed the leaves away and handed her back. She had managed to roll a few times like a fat little worm wrapped tightly in her blanket. Sura remembered it well. It was that day her mother died.

"I knew her when I was a baby," Hyssop said, and reached up to pat Sura's cheek. Hyssop was only a month old when Mother died but a story, when heard enough, becomes a true memory.

Outside, Xur, already as big and strong as a NesGras man has ever been, bristled with energy in the morning light. He held six limber yew saplings, sliced from roots that ran as deep as they were tall. He crouched down to strip away the leaves and bark, and planed the shaft with a rough stone. He ran his palm along the wood and sharpened each spear with a small ax, the tips made as durable as stone in the heat of the fire. He measured each one against the level of the horizon. The spears would fly the course his eyes set. He crouched and sprang, flexed his arm, and took aim at his imagined prey. When he was satisfied with their heft and balance, Xur presented them to his father. Esur lifted each one. Xur watched his father's hands as he passed them back to him. Esur's knobby fingers, frozen in a hunter's grasp, curled toward his palm. He nodded without looking up. The spears were ready.

"Tomorrow," Esur said.

The wind warned them: It was time to move toward the lake across the Wolf Moon mountain range. Xur and Sura would go alone first, entrusted with the search for a refuge from the worst of winter. Zu's quiet, oldest girl died the year before when a brown and rotted tooth had broken off. It started with an ache which she worried with her tongue, and ended in a hallucinatory fever. For two nights she screamed for mercy from the wolves only she could see. *Nothing is lost* they prayed as they buried her. Sura dared not say her name out loud and call death closer. Her own clear eyes and strong teeth, her compact and agile body—the breath that gave her life—could vanish like a sleeping vole snatched by a hawk at water's edge.

Hyssop couldn't walk very far on her weak legs. Bani and Nin were still too young and slow to make the journey to find a place unoccupied by other hunters. The NesGras and the Wolf Moon, their sometimes allies, made a tacit agreement long ago—whoever got there first could stay the winter. If the Wolf Moon were already there, the NesGras had to look elsewhere.

Bani ran in a wide circle to show his speed. "Take me with you," he said.

"Good-bye, Bani." He shrugged off Sura's hugs and Xur's attempt to pat him on the head. They turned to the path toward the mountains. Bani pouted and folded his arms across his chest and stamped his feet and refused to return their smiles and waves. "Next time, Bani. We promise." He shook his head and tossed his dark hair from side to side. "Yes, we promise, beaver," teased Xur, knowing the reference to Bani's new front teeth would make him jump up and down in irritation.

"You are a skunk, Xur," Bani said as they quickened their pace. "No, a skunk smells better."

When he got no reaction from Xur he tried his sister.

"You are a porcupine, Sura, an ugly porcupine. That's why no one can hug you."

"Bye, Bani." They laughed. They knew that he, and Nin, and Hyssop, all with the same big, white front teeth that made their narrow faces look even smaller, would take up their games as soon as they were out of sight.

Brother and sister carried the light spears that Xur made. Each carried a sturdy stick to dig up roots, flaked knives to disjoint game, and flint hammers to smash bones. They headed for the edge of the tree line and looked for mushrooms and tubers they could bury on the long trail and retrieve on the way back. They climbed the rock-strewn incline with ease and grace. Xur's nascent beard was just beginning to show at his jaw, and his shoulders had broadened in the last year. He was nearly a head taller than his sister, and his new strength made him seem so certain and proud. Now he slept with the men apart from the children who huddled at Mina's campfire.

They could still hear the raucous sounds of the children carried on the cool morning air. The last she saw of Bani, Mina was wagging one finger in his face while keeping one reassuring hand on his shoulder. Then she and Xur turned a curve of the mountain and they were alone.

They walked until dark, made a small fire, wrapped themselves in their blankets, and cradled by the ground, fell immediately to sleep. They moved on again before dawn. By mid-morning, black clouds hovered over the high plateau ahead, and the rain slanted like smeared charcoal on a wall of air. Still, the wind blew at their backs, the sun warmed their shoulders, and the earth made way beneath their feet. What prowled beyond their sight and hearing? What watchful eyes and pricked ears followed their tracks? Their scent was carried before them as a warning to the dangers that dared not cross their path. They were young and had each other, and they believed that the past, which gave them health and life, was also an omen for their future. Their mother had not come back to claim them, content to succor the little spirits of her dead infants. Sura saw her mother's campfire in the night sky and was caught between wanting her mother close to her again and dreading that her mother's grief might snatch her away.

"Do you dream of Mother, Xur?"

As he always did, he chewed on her questions a while before he answered.

"Yes," he said.

"What do you dream?"

Without slowing his stride, Xur studied a point in the distance as if the images from his sleep appeared there.

"She tells me stories."

Sura didn't wait for Xur to tell her what stories, impatient to share her own nighttime visions.

"I dream that she is my sister. Or a child I'm supposed to watch. Or she is me then not me. I remember she is my mother though she forgets. Or it is I who forgets…."

Xur stopped. "Listen, Sura. Do you hear that?"

"No," she said.

"May be thunder…or falling rocks."

"Xur, who tends her fire when she's with us?"

"Ask Mina." Xur waved his hand, a signal to move forward and focus on what lay ahead. "Dream stories are better with a full stomach," he added.

She had asked Mina, who told her instead of a long-ago mother who held her dead child until they both turned to stone. She pointed out a round formation jutting from a hill across the valley, and if the waning light played on the surrounding rocks just so, one could make out the features of mother and child. Sura didn't want to hear another story, she was ashamed to admit, that didn't make sense to her, and didn't answer the question. She wanted her mother's tender living breath on her cheek, to sleep near a hearth that gave off light and warmth, and if it failed, could be ignited again.

"My daughter," her mother's living voice whispered long ago, "see what she has made," and she showed a garment crudely knotted by a child's hand. She tried to feel her mother's fingers pulling a splinter from her foot or rubbing a childhood wound with salve. In sleep, a clear vision of her mother returned, while the comfort of her touch was lost. Mother's face was a soft-edged reflection, floating on the water's surface, blurred by the gentlest breeze. The longing stung like a drink of saltwater that burned your throat and left you thirstier than before.

Sura knew it was more than just missing her mother. Soon she would leave her NesGras family. Her father and his brothers would remain together, complete in a silent bond, for as long as they lived. Esur, Rosh, and Ququr brought their women to the NesGras hearth, where their own sons would remain, and their daughters would be dispersed among the friendly clans of the Huul, the Wolf Moon, and the Willow. The appearance of her menstrual blood brought Sura's childhood to a close. She would live with her husband's clan, no longer a NesGras, her father's mark subsumed by a new identity. She tried to think like the adult she was expected to be, to learn where one could walk and where one could not. The silence of the hills allowed her too much time to wonder what might come next. And not enough time to prepare for the inevitable.

Xur interrupted her reverie. "Sura," he whispered.

A red doe grazed at the bottom of a hollow. "When I call you, go over there."

She strained to hear him. "Why?"

"Because I need you to help me bring the deer back."

Sura regarded the steep precipice.

"What if the deer won't come back with us?"

Xur smiled and walked to the rocky ledge. He hunched his shoulders and rotated them back, then ran for no other reason than to feel the power of his legs pumping against the ground. Xur stopped and turned back to look at his sister, and still smiling, placed his bundle of tools down along-side his sleeping robe. Carrying three spears, he jumped to a lower ledge without making a sound.

A damp breeze played across Sura's bare shoulders. She unrolled an elk skin and looped it over the stretched and tanned hide she wore tightly wound under her arms. A blade swung from a cord at her waist. A pouch held the hand ax she used to cut fibers for twine that was stronger than horsehair. Her digging stick was a support and a weapon. Except for the new spears, and the blade that was a gift from Xur, she made all that she wore and carried.

Sura dropped the handful of bilberries she gathered and the wind blew them away. The tracks across this landscape that seemed so clear to Xur were invisible to her. She knew her directions from the rising and setting sun and could hold to the stars on clear nights. This day grew dark, and she would have to rely on Xur to find their way back.

A late afternoon rainstorm was coming close. Flocks of black birds veered overhead cawing and caviling over the approaching night. Sura heard the rumble of thunder. She saw no lightning, and though the smell of rain was strong, it had not started to fall. She scrambled to where Xur left his tools and looked down. The rough walls of the mountains encircled a dappled green valley. Late afternoon shadows shifted with the rising wind, scattering the rays of the lowering sun through swift moving clouds. Stones skipped down the walls from where her toes curled over the edge. She called, "Xur?" She moved to the ledge below and called again. She kept her voice low. Still she felt foolish. What if she sent the deer scurrying? She saw almost nothing. Was Xur playing a trick on her? How much time had passed since he spoke to her? Holding on to the exposed roots of an oak, she descended farther. The lower she went, the colder it was. Shivering, she searched the darkening rift.

Xur, where are you?

Lightning spit across the sky and thunder jarred the air right after. The storm was moving closer. Rain splattered in large drops all around her. The sky flashed again and she saw him, moving slowly, his back against the mountain wall, his face against the wind. Above him he heard Sura call him and tightened his mouth against an answer. He would scold her later. The doe's ears and tail lifted, alert to danger, frozen in the sudden flare of light. Xur tried for the part of the ledge wide enough for him to heave his spear. He focused on the trajectory the spear would take. Soon the shadows would obscure the valley floor and hunger would have the advantage. It was not hunger that told Xur to take one more step onto an outcrop of sandy stone that had started to break away. Leaning forward, Xur positioned the spear above his right shoulder, his fingers gripping the wooden shaft at its widest point. He held his left arm straight out in front of him as counterweight. He shifted farther toward the edge. Below, the deer sniffed at the air and began to move away from her grazing spot. Her hide bristled. Her chest rose in a graceful arc as she prepared to run. Xur aimed at the deer's exposed neck. He drew the spear back and hurled it with all of his strength. The narrow outcrop where he stood ripped from the mountain wall with a roar. The thrust of the spear flipped the deer over onto her side; her legs ran on the air. Like dirt flung from an invisible hand, Xur hurtled headlong down the cliff, hitting his head and shoulder on the rocks before landing hard on his right leg. He, like the deer, quivered and was still.

Sura clambered to the ledge where her brother lay face down, his left arm twisted behind him. Carefully she turned him over. The bone below the knee of his right leg showed blue where it was driven through the flesh. For a startled instant, Sura did not recognize him. His face in the shadows was covered with blood and debris. She looked closer. The thin flesh of his brow above his right eye was scraped away. Sura knelt over Xur's body. She had to act quickly. She took a long breath, and pushed her panic aside. She put her ear to his chest and listened for his heartbeat. She had to stanch the blood from his brow. She pulled the wrap from her shoulders and tore off strips with her teeth. She wound a strip tightly around Xur's head. She moved her hands down along his spine searching for fatal wounds. She removed a leather cord from her waist and tied it tightly above his knee. She grasped his leg above his ankle and below his knee. She had helped her father set broken bones many times before, but never by herself. A long moan rumbled from deep in Xur's chest. An animal sound eating from inside. Sura manipulated the protruding shinbone back into place, imperfectly rejoining the broken ends. She cleaned the area around the open wound and used the rest of her elkskin wrap to cover the gap in his flesh. She shattered her digging stick against the rocks to make a splint. Sura took two spears that lay near him and stuck them into the ground beside him. She covered him with his blanket, and placed her own on top of his, praying that the night would, somehow, miss the chance to take him.

"Don't die, Xur," she whispered before leaving him. She began her ascent in the last of the twilight. Cold mud slipped down the valley wall toward the ledge where her brother lay.

CHAPTER THREE

LOST

Sura followed the path north. Outlined by the dim light of the moon, slumbering volcanoes formed a barrier around the hills and valleys. She tried to swallow her fear when flying insects buzzed in her ears, caught in her hair, flew into her eyes and nose, and down her throat. Mice crossed her path, skittering just above the ground, their tails straight out, squealing an alarm to other small creatures of the night. Sounds of whirring and rustling, howls and hoots, gave terrible voice to the darkness. She stretched her hands out in front of her to keep from stumbling over unseen rocks that tore the soles of her feet, bruised her shins, and scraped her flesh against the jutting, indifferent scales of stone.

The rain clouds closed over the North Star and veiled the face of the moon. The rest was black. She walked into a mountain wall and stopped. Stunned, she changed directions. Sura tried to feel her way along the landscape they had passed only hours before. Time eluded her. They had traveled two days' distance from camp to reach the place where Xur had fallen. The path they took gently dropped to the foothills of the mountains. To get home she would have to climb, yet she felt the oblique slope of the land pulling her down. Even the wet air moved more slowly. The pelting rain seemed warmer, less punishing. She needed to get her bearings and find the path back home. When the rain stopped and the clouds cleared, the path would find her. *If the rain stops*, she thought.

Wings snapped open and whipped the air above her head. Sura held her breath. An owl, gliding silently by, swooped down and plucked up a mouse. With a short flurry of squeals and a rustle of feathers, she headed back to her roost. Sura felt as vulnerable as the mouse and prayed for help to the spirit that gave the owl eyes to see through the blackness. The path she searched for was swallowed by the night. Already far away, the owl hooted as the quiet before dawn spread over the invisible landscape.

The cold made her shiver violently. Her waterlogged foot coverings had fallen off somewhere along the way. Her soaked shift was slicked with ice against her skin. She pulled her knees to her chest and wrapped her arms around them. The jagged half of her digging stick lay broken on some rocky tumble. Only her pouch and blade remained. Everything else was with Xur. *Why did I leave him? What good am I to him cold and lost? Blind. No tool, no weapon. Forgive me, Mother, for losing your son.*

The night sky faded to gray. Sura gasped as the sun rose with blinding brightness from behind the NesGras mountain that she faced. She murmured, "Does the sun rise in the west today?" as her body folded down to the ground, numbed by exhaustion into a deep, bitter sleep.

Light radiated through her eyelids. She dreamed of a red landscape. She heard the voices of her father, her uncles, her brothers. "Sura, you're back." She smelled meat roasting and heard the comforting sounds of morning in her camp. Sleep receded and the voices changed shape. She snapped awake.

Not far from her stood three young men. She jumped to her feet and clutched the only weapon she had—the small quartz blade. Her hair, normally dressed with oil and coiled into plaits, fanned out and up into a tangled web of brambles and insects. She was scratched and bruised and bumpy from insect bites. She stood. A sprained ankle made her list to one side. Her hands bled from falling in the dark. Gray dust covered her. Only her eyes showed that she was human.

One of the men spoke. "Ho," said Naki. "A girl."

They circled her and ducked their heads, studying her as if she were a strange plant sprung up from the muddy ground.

"What's your name?"

"Are you alone?"

Was she alone?

"Are you hurt?" Naki raised his voice, and they all three moved closer to her. Sura sank down on her knees and dropped the blade, green and veined like a leaf, into her lap.

"Are you hurt?" Naki asked again, softly this time.

Sura raised her eyes only high enough to see their leather-shod feet planted in a loose semicircle, close enough to show her they knew that she posed no threat, and far enough away from her to signal they meant no harm.

"Yes. A little." Sura's tears zigzagged in narrow rivulets down her grimy face.

"But my brother is hurt. Very badly. I left him to find our father. I got lost instead."

Naki knelt so that his face was level with hers. "That's a bad thing." His two companions nodded. "A very bad thing."

"I need to get back to my brother. Can you help me? Please."

Sura brushed the back of her hand across her eyes. Muddy tears streaked her face. She told them about the deer and Xur's terrible fall, and the sky that shut its face to her. How in the dark and the rain she ended up *here*.

"I thought I could find my way back to my father," she said, "and instead, I've left him to die."

They clucked their tongues. "We see, we see," they said, and looked in every direction except at her to show their good intentions and their respect for her dilemma.

"Your brother fell," they repeated, "but you don't know where. And he may be dead."

"No, not dead! He's alive, and I have to get him back to our people."

"Who are your people?" they asked.

"The NesGras, from the mountains of the Huul," and she pointed east where the sun cut through the clouds and morning mist. "My father is Esur."

"We are people of the Huul too," said Naki. "The Nir." And he pointed west, toward the distant, blue-green sea.

"If you are Nir," said Sura, "then I've gone very far."

"Not so far," he said. "We are still in a valley of the Huul."

They stepped away from her. What should they do? Sura wanted them to retrace her trail back to Xur and help bring him back to their camp. After all, they were members of the clans who traded tools, food, ornaments. More than that, they shared bloodlines; their pasts were linked to the time of their ancient grandfathers. They glimpsed at Sura's swollen ankle. Under the dirt, they could see her mark. NesGras, the unyielding and stolid clan who were once their enemies, avoided now to keep an uneasy peace. This girl who tumbled from her mountain posed no danger to them.

"Look at her," said Naki. "She has no weapons. She doesn't even have a stick to lean on. She can't read the sky for directions." Naki's brother Dzo was about to remind him that no one could read the sky on a cloud-covered night, but Naki went on. "If we leave her here alone, she will die. Is it the Nir way to let strangers die?"

In answer, they pointed to heavy, white clouds that were chasing the sun. "Snow is coming."

Naki's face took on an angle of determination. "Yes, and we've come before the snow." He turned to his brother. "We will help her. You," he said to his cousin, "go back to our camp and tell our mothers where we're going."

"What should I say, Naki?"

"Tell them we are helping a brother find his way home."

Sura led Naki and Dzo back toward the trampled path she made the night before. In the morning light, nothing looked familiar. No dark, remembered outline resembled the fragrant cedars that were now stippled in shades of gold and green. She was hungry and tired; to be in the company of young men, without her family, made her feel awkward and uncertain. They did nothing to make her afraid, averting their eyes when either of them spoke. Still, her boldness surprised her as she led them across a landscape that she had never seen in daylight. Naki and Dzo gradually moved to walk beside her, studying the ground and gently nudging her across the broken signs of last night's reckless course. The sun moved from behind the clouds only to retreat again like a mischievous spirit hiding its light, watching without watching over them. She was glad for the company; their voices soothed her, the nearness of their sympathetic faces and strong bodies comforted her. Without turning her head, she noticed their black hair and their skin, like hers, browned by the sun. *Nir, the people who live by the sea, are helping me. What do you think of that, Grandfather?*

She remembered the old man's mystifying stories about other clans who shared their land. "Nir," he said, glowering across the campfire to make sure they were thoroughly frightened, "devoured the children of the Willow, the Wolf Moon, and the NesGras. They ate the livers of young girls and swallowed whole the hearts of hunters." He spit on the ground to emphasize the bitter taste. Her aunt Mina and her mother, who carried memories of Nir kinship, assured the children, after the old man had fallen asleep, that his stories were more false than true. Sura now wondered which parts were true and which were an old man's fantasy.

"Girl," said Naki as he lightly laid his hand on her shoulder. "Let's stop for a while," and he gathered the fingers of his right hand close together and gestured toward his mouth—*eat*.

Sura stared at him, instinctively covering the side she thought her liver would be. Clutching what was left of her leather shift to her body, she abruptly sat on the ground.

"Good," said Naki with a puzzled look on his face. "Good," he repeated as he motioned toward the ground. "Sit."

Dzo motioned to a nearby shrub with a rapid shift of his eyes. Naki gave a little nod, and they both ran toward the shrub. A big, gray hare popped out suddenly and all three were off, running first to the left and then to the right, swerving from side to side. The hare, as if to signal it was in on the game, flattened its ears. In a flash, Naki was upon it. A blow from his hand axe to the unfortunate hare's skull ended its exciting but short life. Dzo and Naki carried it back to where Sura sat, her hunger sitting like rough stones in her stomach. Naki pulled dry moss and two pieces of flint from his kit and started a fire. "Thank you," they all said, and they bowed to the southern sky where warmth resides. Dzo slipped the animal's fur from its flesh in one fluid motion, like removing a close-fitting garment. He brought the animal's still-warm flesh to his face and breathed in deeply. He slit the animal down its pink belly and filled his mouth with the deep-red liver. Naki took a bite, then passed its glossy, bloody heart to Sura while Dzo improvised a spit over the fire. The anticipation made her stomach rattle like a gourd. She swallowed the rest of the heart, and the sharp, little stones inside her growled, then fell silent. She rose and gathered the coiled ferns and nuts that clustered around a yellow-leafed tree. She pushed them inside the cavity of the hare and secured it to the spit. Not enough food to sustain them very long, but enough for today.

They ate and walked until the sun set and made camp. In the morning, Sura drank from a clear puddle and was startled by her reflection. She looked up. Naki was concentrating on whittling a toothpick. She splashed the water on her face. "Before it freezes," she said. She looked at Naki again. This time, Naki couldn't return to his whittling fast enough before Sura caught his glance. *Why should I care if he thinks I'm ugly?*

"Is this the place?" asked Naki as Sura searched the ground beyond the mountain ledge. The heavy rainfall had washed away signs of Xur's presence. Only the antlered skull of the deer remained. Her other bones, sucked clean of their marrow by scavengers, lay scattered and broken on the valley floor. A scrap of leather and piles of white ash, the scat of hyenas, were all that remained of the dinner they had made and the blanket Sura had left with Xur. She shivered harder at the memory of its warmth. Wind from the north, sharp and cold, whipped the remnants of her clothing. The rain turned to hail, which collected in the jagged recesses of the mountain-sides; hail, they all were aware, that was not melting. Snow would follow, maybe not in a day, but soon. No amount of will could stop her teeth from clattering. She had to make a decision: to take off alone and search for Xur and the rest of her family or follow Naki and Dzo. She looked up at the bleak and unforgiving sky. The two young men examined her face for a sign. Sura turned to face the biting wind. Naki and Dzo fell in beside her. Together they started their journey to the shell-cracked shore of the Nir.

Sleet and rain obscured the rising and setting of the sun. Day was no warmer than night when they took shelter in the mouth of a cave, built a fire, and lay down in exhaustion. Sura no longer questioned her judgment in leaving Xur. She knew she was a fool who could not find her way. On the day they arrived at Naki and Dzo's camp, the sun came out and stayed to warm the air. Naki and Dzo pranced with renewed energy for the last few miles. Sura broke her melancholy trudge and dashed to catch up with them.

The circular compound lay in an expansive clearing. Chopped-down trees and shrubs were piled tall around the perimeter. Shelters and hearths surrounded the blackened circle of a doused bonfire. People drew excitedly around them as they entered. More children than Sura had ever seen rushed up to touch her. Giggling and whooping, they ran dizzy circles around her and Naki and Dzo. Two slender girls, about the same age as Sura, smug under their ochre-and- charcoal paint, looked at Sura with narrowed eyes. She felt ashamed under their gaze, like a mangy animal whose only adornment was the dust and burrs of the journey. The young men had each contributed parts of their own clothing to keep her from freezing. Nothing came together to indicate who or what she was. She looked like a boy without a mother, a mad traveler without a clan or a hearth for shelter. Sura searched her mind for an appropriate greeting. She dredged up an image of her aunt Mina instructing her what she should say to strangers. She could see Mina's hands, her moving lips, her focused eyes. Why was she deaf to the memory?

Some of the adults were now coming up to her, pointing to her hair, her feet, touching her clothing, trying to peek beneath her tattered shift. They half-hoped that the figure before them would somehow be more than just a hungry, tired girl. Yet, their laughter warmed her. Sura wrapped Dzo's too-big shawl around her, prayed for courage, and raised her eyes to meet them.

While Naki and Dzo accompanied Sura in her search to find Xur, Naki's cousin was regaling their camp with the story of the lost NesGras girl. The Nir were mystified. How did she convince Dzo and Naki to go along with her? Speculation raged among the people as they went about their daily chores.

"Those boys are fools," some said while they sharpened obsidian blades in the sun. "They have insulted our spirit ancestors and we will suffer."

"Dzo and Naki were kind to help a stranger," others said as they gathered roots at the edge of the forest. "This will bring us good luck."

They said, "She is no mere girl." Their breaths caught in their throats as scorched seeds popped in the fire. "She is an evil spirit leading our sons to death."

"Or worse."

"Or worse." Someone always agreed.

CHAPTER FOUR

BREATHE

A rising sun touched Xur's face and he stirred. Heavy stones seemed to press down on his lids. He wanted to sleep, to drift back to oblivion and not face the pain he felt gathering in his head and leg. A crow alighted on his chest and took a tentative peck at his shoulder. The touch struck him like a burning spear, hot and sharp, and pulsed through his body so fiercely, he did not know which part of him was torn and broken and which was whole. *Breathe*, he said, willing himself to confront the pain. *Breathe*. His chest rose and fell. He moved his fingers, then his hands and arms. It took all of his strength and concentration to open his eyes just enough to see the daylight. He raised his head from the stiff angle of his neck and looked to check if his legs and feet were still attached to his body. He fought back the pain, locating and diminishing it, so that it did not overwhelm him. He remembered leaving his family—*was it yesterday?* He remembered ascending the mountain with Sura. Had the mountain turned upside down and fallen on him?

Xur pushed up on his elbows, then forced himself to sit up, his palms flat on the ground to steady himself. He closed his eyes and tried to think beyond the throbbing in his head. He leaned forward slowly so that he could grasp his wounded leg above the knee with his hands. Xur tugged at the tight bandage that his sister made and lifted the edge. He inspected his splinted leg. The effort exhausted him. He slept until a low roar he thought was thunder, yet sounded close enough to a lion's irritable rumble, fully woke him. The sun was still in the eastern sky. In the west, rain clouds gathered against a white sky. The wound made by his broken bone was already forming a thick scab. "Well done, Sura," he said aloud. The cool mud that drifted down the steep hillside had formed a cradle around his head and body. He knew he could not lie there another night or the hunter would become the prey.

Nothing is lost, he prayed, to bolster his courage and to rid himself, whenever he heard thunder, of the imagined lion that would attack and trap Xur's spirit behind its glowering eyes.

He rolled over and crawled slowly toward the rim of the overhang that broke his fall. The deer that he struck with his spear still lay in the valley below, or rather the hide, skeleton, and antlers lay there. The deer was now an empty sack, looted of its contents by hyenas, vultures, and flies. He raised up onto his hands and knees and cried out in pain to the empty sky. He leaned heavily on the returning power of his uninjured arm to stand. Sura's blanket lay on the ground to mark the place he returned to life.

He started down the sharp incline of the rock face toward the narrow route between two plateaus. It was not the path that he and Sura had used to arrive at this place, and though a greater distance, it would keep him on a flatter terrain. Sura, he was certain, would leave him only to go for help, and it was the path his father would take to come for him.

Xur pushed his way through the mountain corridor. Rain fell in big splats on flat surfaces and streaked the yellow canyon walls that enclosed a space wide enough for his arms to span. Leaning heavily on his good leg, avoiding landing too hard on the other, he grew wearier and more disoriented with each step. He struggled on for miles, fighting to keep his balance so that he wouldn't fall and be unable to rise before snow or rain could fill the narrow pass.

It was in that very place not long before that he killed an elk. His father and his uncles had maneuvered the animal into the trap where its wide antlers made it impossible to turn around in the tapering slot. Xur fought the thick feeling in his head to remember that day. He saw himself scramble down the mountain wall to face the elk that swung its massive antlers from side to side, sending loosened rocks chattering to the ground with each strike. Xur mouthed a prayer of thanks as his spear pierced the elk's great heart, its tall front legs folding beneath its weight to kneel in surprised obeisance before the stronger spirit. The kill seemed effortless, and Xur congratulated himself on his superior hunting skill as he planted the final spear in the beast's still-pulsing throat. Had Xur allowed himself too much pride in his strength and in his keen aim? Had he disdained the elk for succumbing to death too easily? Sura's cape, now wrapped around his leg, was once on the living back of that elk. The blade in his kit was a piece of the antler that the elk futilely struck against the mountain walls. For the first time, Xur felt the fear and helplessness in common with his prey. The blood he tasted in his mouth was his own, and the spirit that clamored in his heart was the elk's that gave its life in that mountain pass not long ago.

"He's alive, Bha!" Bani said to his father.

Xur felt his brother's hands caressing his face. He heard the voices of his father and uncles. He tasted the liquid trickling between his lips. Pain seared his arm and leg as he was lifted onto a pallet made of leather and wood. He hovered above the ground, awake or in a dream, he could not tell.

"Bha knew you were hurt and led us here to you," said Bani, squeezing Xur's hand as he ran alongside him.

"Mina marked the ground where you left. She said the mark would help you and Sura find your way back. . . ."

Sura. Her name jolted him.

"Where is Sura, Bani?"

Bani's smile fell.

"Xur, she was with you."

I've lost Sura, he thought he cried out, but his open mouth made no sound.

When Xur woke again, he was inside a low-ceilinged cave. Moist air was visible in the light from the fire. Bani slept next to him, his child's body pressed against Xur's side. Mina, silhouetted by the light of a torch wedged between two stones, was on her knees, painting on the rocky wall. Shells filled with color sat beside her: yellow gorse, green privet, black elder, and deep-blue indigo. A figure on the wall floated with outstretched arms, his legs held stiffly together. A chimera with the face and claws of a bear and the body of a man hovered over him. A small figure floated like smoke away from the larger ones. The flickering light on the craggy walls and the pounding in his skull made the forms lurch and stumble. A smoldering pyramid of juniper animated their dance. Xur began to focus as the fire died down. The visions stilled, and reality crept in like sunlight burning off the fog. Mina's medicine worked on Xur's broken bones, and while no chimera had injured him, he regretted the carelessness and pride that brought him back here without his sister.

"Mina?"

"She's safe, Xur. Rest."

Since they'd found him, Mina neither slept nor ate. She focused only on caring for Xur and on the rituals for the children of her dead sister. When her exhortations to the spirits of the air were exhausted, she invoked the very mother of life herself and took Xur to the belly of the earth, to a cave in NesGras Huul. For three days and nights, she labored. When Xur's fever cooled, she took a vessel of clear water, and just as carefully as she had applied the painted prayer to the cave wall, she washed it all away. Her prayer dispatched, she rested and waited for a response.

Xur dreamt he was running with his spear held high. He heard the laughter of his family all around him. The wind carried him. The celerity of his legs defied the ground, and a thunderous clamor of hooves beat the earth in front of him. When he emerged from his dream, it was light and he was outside the cave. Everyone was awake except for Mina, who, streaked with the colors from her paint, slept on the bare earth.

Untreated injuries like Xur's would rot the flesh while the body burned from within. Death alone would break the fever. Esur's compress of dried and powdered oak bark had stopped the bleeding. Wrapped with twine—long shafts of dry, summer grass—he untied and retied the binding, careful not to break the thick scab that formed over the wound. His words were in his skilled hands. They prescribed the cure, and the children watched and learned. Xur sat up, and Bani ran to his side with willow tea. Xur sipped the bitter liquid, and the throbbing in his head slowed. Esur turned away and walked to the outer rim of their encampment. He took up a flint he had not worked since Xur was found and with a sharp blow returned to his tool making. Xur watched his father from where he rested and thanked him in his heart for giving him life again.

The sky hung white and heavy, so close they could almost touch the cold. The time to move was narrowing. When the mountain passes filled with snow and ice, it would be too late. The hope of wintering at the fecund lake valley to their west diminished. Their food stores were low. The gazelle migration route was to the north, and the early freeze meant they were already on the run. Without Xur and Sura, their strength was diminished. One big animal—an aurochs, a horse, or a bear—could see them through the winter. The band was small and did not require much food. A good thing since it would be hard to bring down a large and nimble animal with only three able-bodied men. Esur, Rosh, and Ququr made short forays to look for small game, leaving Mina alone to care for Rosh's pregnant wife Zu, Xur with his broken leg, and to keep watch over the children. Every solution brought new problems. In the winter, the bears hibernated; lions and wolves, moving in packs, did not.

Ququr heard the signal first—a crow's *caw caw* and the long, high-pitched *awooo* of a wolf. Two lone hunters from the Wolf Moon clan were approaching.

"Show yourselves," he shouted, and they stepped within the circle of the camp.

The young men bowed toward Esur, and then to all the other adults in the camp. One of the men looked at the ground while the older of the two studied the air above the NesGras heads. He spoke as if he had repeated the message many times in his head before giving it voice.

"An old one of the Nir asked us to carry these words to you: 'The lost NesGras girl is safe. When the snow in the lowland is melted, the clans of the Huul will meet at the cave of the goats. She will be there.'" They crossed their hands over their chests, which is meant to say *Should we live through winter.*

Esur spoke first. "You have taken great care of these words. Thank you."

"We are glad to bring them to you," and they bowed and nodded one more time.

Then, formalities being over, the rest shouted their thanks, pounded the men on their backs, and offered them food and a place at their campfire for as long as they wished to stay, as was the way of the Huul.

CHAPTER FIVE

ALU

In the three days Naki and Dzo were alone with Sura, she had grown and morphed in the minds of the Nir waiting for them to come back. When they entered, even the boys' cousin was surprised to discover that Sura was not the inhuman giant they were creating in their minds. In the excitement of a real, live stranger among them, their feelings of dread melted away, at least for most.

"This is my mother, Alu," said Naki, indicating a lean woman sitting stiffly erect between two girls. "My sister Tehil," he said, "and my cousin, Zamia."

Before Sura could turn to look at Naki he was gone, and the flap from the tent opening fluttered down behind her. Across the fire burning in the center, Alu's eyes shone round and yellow. Naki's unsmiling female relatives stared at her. Unlike Naki, who spoke in an incessant burble to her from the first moment of their meeting, the girls turned their backs to her. Whispering to each other, they cast baleful glances at her over their shoulders.

"I'm Sura . . . NesGras," she finally said.

Alu nodded and pushed a shell toward her filled with water, fragrant with lavender and hyssop. The girls were dipping a chamois cloth into their shells and cleaning themselves. She was expected to do the same. Sura passed the wet cloth over her wind-chapped face. The warmth of the water, the bouquet of the tiny, purple flowers, and the glow of the fire soothed her. She dipped and wrung out the cloth and rubbed her body from her neck to her feet. She poured the last drop over her hair and was combing it through with her fingers when she noticed the three faces suspended above her like disapproving moons. But when food was placed before her, she ate it so quickly she could not have told if it was vegetable or meat, liquid or solid, her self-consciousness obliterated by her hunger. She murmured her thanks and Alu nodded again, her mouth so tightly closed it looked like it was sewn shut. Sura was confused. Was she unwelcome, or was this the Nir way to greet a stranger? Exhaustion and the warmth and comfort of the shelter against the cold overtook her, and she fell at once into a deep sleep.

In the morning, Sura awoke to find Alu gone and Tehil and Zamia taking turns carefully applying designs on each other's cheeks and fore-heads with a stick of charcoal. In the dimness of the shelter, the ochre base on their faces and shoulders was a deep crimson. Sura watched in fasci-nation. When they looked in her direction, their smiles dropped and they lowered their eyelids so slowly, Sura thought they would fall unconscious just to blot out the sight of her.

Sura rose and left them to what she assumed was their beautifying. Out in the morning dampness, the other Nir greeted her. "There," they said, pointing to a worn path leading to the outer rim of the camp. Sura ran up the path, followed by the laughter of the adults and the shouts of the children who were proud to be old enough to no longer pee on the ground where they stood.

Back at the center of the camp, Sura looked around her. A man, older than her father, sat cleaning his teeth with a twig, the ends of which were frayed into a fringe of soft bristles. A younger man gravely sucked on the enormous shinbone of a horse. Stripped of meat some time ago, his tongue explored for the last of the marrow through a small hole bored in the middle. Kneeling behind him, a young woman groomed his hair. Unwelcome creatures lurking in his abundant locks were pinched between her thumb and forefinger and snapped into the campfire. A gray-haired woman smiled broadly at Sura, showing teeth worn nearly to the gums. She worked a segment of deer hide, stretching and rotating it between her hands and her clenched jaws. The woman motioned to Sura to sit down beside her and handed her a softened piece of hide without breaking the rhythm of her task or narrowing her smile. She pointed with her chin at Sura's shift, hanging crooked and torn.

"For me?"

The woman nodded.

"I have nothing for you, Grandmother."

The woman set her work down and put her rough hand to Sura's cheek. "I need nothing," she said.

Days and nights passed. Sura knew deep winter was bearing down, and it would be a long time before she saw her family again. She tried to show her gratitude by hiding her tears and helping the gatherers who shared their food with her. She wasn't afraid—it was loneliness that gnawed at her heart. The Nir sang and laughed and pointed to the sky the same as her own NesGras family did. They greeted her in the same language, though filled with mysterious observations that completely eluded her. Yet, she ached to take Hyssop in her lap, to see her father, silent and still, at the edge of their small camp, or to hear Nin once again, weeping without tears that Bani got more to eat than he did.

On an afternoon after a heavy storm, Sura ventured north into the denser forest to look for acorns. Massive bracket fungus, fed by the cold, dank air, grew high over her head on the trunk of an oak. Sura stretched for a stout branch and hoisted herself high enough to reach the giant mushroom. Her musky catch tucked under her arm, Sura prepared to jump to the ground. She paused as the voices of Tehil and Zamia became audible. The girls neared the tree where Sura balanced on an upper branch. Tehil and Zamia stooped to fill their pouches with lichen and borage. *Borage*, thought Sura, *would heal Xur's wounds*. She determined to gather borage now so she wouldn't be without it again. She leapt to the ground, causing Tehil and Zamia to drop what they gathered and yelp in fright.

"You stupid mud hen," they shrieked at her.

"You silly, skittering squirrels," she said.

"You smell like rancid oil!"

"You smell"—Sura searched for the most putrid odor—"like dead buzzard livers," she added.

Tehil said, "Since you came, our tent reeks of your bowels."

"Yes," they said, "go back where you came from!"

"I'll go where I want!"

"Where is that? You can't even find your way. . . ."

"Home," said Sura, and burst into sobs. "I don't want to be with you. I miss Esur and Mina, and my family. And I am going back."

Sura's chin shook with great effort to control her tears. *A NesGras adult wailing like an infant.* She felt ashamed. She would leave, and if she died, well, it would be better to die closer to home, to go back over the mountains that formed a barrier between where she stood and all that she knew. The wind blew harder and the cold stones rebuked her. Sura turned in a circle.

Tehil and Zamia glanced at each other. What was she looking for? Had their hearts grown so small that they would affront the first tenet of the Huul: welcome the stranger?

"Don't cry, Sura," they said. "You will go back. You'll see, as soon as it's warm again."

"Look." They picked up some spiraled fern buds dried and frozen in the detritus that collected in the roots of the tree. "They look like snail shells."

Sura gazed at them and sniffled. "They do."

"They are very good to eat."

"When they are green," said Sura, trying to compose herself.

Sura began to pick up the spilled foodstuffs. In a conciliatory gesture, she placed her prized bracket fungus in their pile, climbed the tree again, and pulled away another one. Tehil, not to be outdone, climbed another oak and raided a knothole for a squirrel's winter store. When the squirrel saw Tehil in its larder, it jerked away, dithering and chattering at the girls in annoyance. Zamia, imitating the squirrel, picked up a moldy acorn and flipped it into her mouth. "Not fit for squirrels," she said and spat it out. Sura flapped her arms.

"Mud hens are very good to eat," said Tehil. And to their surprise, they laughed.

Walking back to camp in the gathering dusk, their arms linked and their back slings filled with foraged nuts and mushrooms, they sang a song about the newly fallen snow. They marveled at the complex symmetry of the flakes that caught in their hair before melting into tiny drops of water.

"They say they are gifts tossed to us from the stars."

"We thank you, but not too many, please," they sang together.

The snow piled on top of their hair, and they imagined that they looked like the pines that grew high in the mountains. They wore their snowy hats all through the encampment until Tehil, entering their shelter first, had hers knocked off by her mother, warning enough for the other girls to shake their hair dry before going inside. That night, as they settled around the fire, huddled comfortably together, Tehil and Zamia named and described every person who lived in their large band. Alu, exasperated beyond her usual ill humor, pulled a stick from the fire and smashed it against the rock wall. A shower of sparks silenced the girls, and knowing better than to further provoke her wrath, they nestled down under their covers, closed their eyes, and fell asleep. And Sura half-dreamed her prayer for Xur:

> *Mother, may there be food tomorrow and fire to keep us warm.*
>
> *Guide Xur to our father.*
>
> Then she touched her hands to her chest,
>
> *Should we live through winter.*

CHAPTER SIX

THE CAIRN

The cold deepened, and the wind blew without ceasing. Naki and the other young men of the camp were often gone for days at a time tracking game. Sometimes, after subsisting on over-wintering tubers and the occasional wild onion, they would return, weary and starving, forced to draw further on the dwindling stores of the camp. Now, except for the few hardy persons who remained outside at night keeping watch, all the families slept within the shelter of caves. Two babies, unable to nurse, died within days of each other. Convulsed by fever, eyes rolled back, their small faces took on a waxy repose, and they were gone without a cry. Sura grieved along with the families of these untried spirits. She wept, remembering children from her own family taken in seasons past. She suffered from the loss and separation from her people who bore the intolerable sting of winter in another place too far away.

The father of one of the dead babies ran outside the cave. Cursing, he picked up the heaviest stones and hurled them into the face of the wind. "Show yourself. Show yourself to me, and I will kill you with my bare hands!" The wind, mocking his rage, blocked the thrust of the stones. They fell weakly to the ground, rolling across the landscape like pebbles. Fearing the wind could take greater vengeance still, the people in the cave scrambled to bring him inside.

"Your child's tender soul will become a flower of the field in the spring," they soothed. And they came to believe it was true.

The Nir moved slowly, following a small herd of horses searching for fodder and fresh water. They traveled away from the sea toward higher ground. There the air was drier, and though the shrubs were less abundant, the trees grew taller. They were returning to a cave that they had occupied many winters before. Perhaps the tall trees would provide nuts this year. The mystery of the tree's sporadic barrenness eluded them, and they were careful to avoid insulting its bountiful, if capricious, spirit. They came at dusk to the spot where they set up camp and prepared the fires.

Tehil and Zamia came running toward Sura, their faces grim with fear. "We can't find Alu," they said. They left the campsite to look for her, each in a different direction, not daring to travel too far and be caught alone as night fell.

Sura was the first to hear the humming sound. *Was it human?* She warned herself to hasten back to the shelter of the group, yet her curiosity drew her closer. A small fire burned before a cairn of gray stones piled upon a mound of freshly dug earth. Set above the cairn, a seething vessel of nightshade gave off a poisonous vapor. A miniature catafalque bearing two small bundles of sticks was set above the unsavory concoction. *Who or what had died here?* Sura moved closer. A kneeling figure, naked to the waist despite the cold, swayed before the fire.

Sura felt a jolt of terror tear through her body. It was Alu. Sura did not have to know all the ways of the Nir to fear the evil that Alu was invoking.

She moved closer.

"Alu," she said softly, "it's almost dark."

She did not answer. Her eyes were open, staring and unseeing. She continued her keening and raised her arms as if to bathe them in the stench of the rising vapor. Her body slumped to the side as slowly and weightlessly as a dried leaf. Ignoring the impulse to flee, Sura overturned the cairn, sending the rocks and sticks flying. She kicked dirt over the foul-smelling fire and stomped on the sticks until they were broken and scattered on the ground. Dreading the presence of an evil spirit invoked by Alu's magic, Sura recited an incantation: "Mother, protect me from all harm," not daring to allow a breach in her consciousness for the evil to enter her spirit. Her hair stood stiff on her arms and legs and on the back of her neck. She shivered from the cold wind and from the fear that she was straddling a line between the natural world she understood and the spirit world that Alu manipulated but could not ultimately control.

She picked up Alu's body and lifted her in her arms as she would a sleeping child. Without daring to look back, she ran to the shelter that Naki had just finished raising. She lay Alu down, hidden in the darkness. Sura ran in the direction Tehil and Zamia had taken and called them back. She described what she had seen. Tehil began to cry. "Have you noticed the old man with the young woman sitting at the farthest corner of the camp?" she asked Sura.

Sura nodded. "He is my father."

"Two years ago, he took the girl to be his second wife. My mother would not accept it. She raged day and night. Alu was never a soft person, and she grew harder and more bitter. There was no sleep for anyone here. People said that even the animals deep in the forest could not sleep from her wailing and would move to where our hunters would never find them. Finally, my father and the girl—Alu forbids us to say her name—set up their own campfire as far away from Alu as possible. Naki provides her with meat. She is his mother, but he doesn't want to turn away from his father as Alu demands. We try to respect her wishes, yet every day she grows angrier."

Tehil paused to wipe a tear and glance over at her mother, who had not moved since Sura had lain her down.

"If the others find out what she has been doing when she is away from camp," she said, "do you know what will happen? She will be shunned. She will be cast out of the Nir and she will die."

Days passed, and Alu ate less and less. She refused all meat from her children and ate only the weeds that she gathered and kept in a pouch in her apron. Despite this, her strength grew. Her body was as hard as the gnarled root of the oak. Her face was a stone from which her yellow eyes blazed. Her children feared the danger she was creating for herself, while all who saw her feared the evil power she was leading to them.

"Girl," a voice crackled in the dry air. Sura straightened. In her hand, she clutched the feathery, gray-green foliage of the yarrow plant.

"What do you call that?" asked Alu. Sura told her the name.

"What do you use it for?"

"Headache, toothache, fever, insect bites, splinters, bleeding, scalding." Sura recited until Alu stopped her.

"And the oil?" asked Alu.

Sura hesitated. "You have more to learn, I see."

Alu reached into her bag and pulled out a smooth, red branchlet. The leaves were narrow and silvery green.

"It is bitter willow," said Sura. "It soothes pain."

"What else can it do?" asked Alu.

"Compresses made from bitter willow keep wounded flesh from rotting. You can eat the roots to get rid of worms."

"And the catkins?" asked Alu.

Sura began to see what Alu was getting at. She wanted to know how much Sura knew of women's medicine. Among the many things that Mina taught her, one was to keep secrets.

Alu opened a pouch, and Sura smelled the familiar odor of wintergreen.

"Birch is for sore feet." Sura lied.

Alu studied her. "We'll speak again," she said as she turned to go deeper into the surrounding forest. From Sura's earliest memory, she watched Mina attend the people of her band. Mina, and Sura's mother in the years before she weakened, would travel great distances to other camp-sites where their skills would heal the broken and deliver the newborn. She remembered Mina brewing tea from the cones formed by the maturing fruit of the birch to ease the pain that followed childbirth.

Sura could feel the warm presence of Mina beside her now, could hear her say, "Smell this, Sura," as she broke a twig and the penetrating scent would sharpen her breath. Mina collected the fluttery bark, which could be used to kindle a fire even in the rain. The birch twig prodded her memories in a way Alu's questions could not. She was with Xur, and they were children licking the sap off the trunk of the birch in the early days of spring in her high mountain home.

CHAPTER SEVEN

DANCE

The Nir hunters were gone for three days. Even Alu seemed to come out of her self-imposed trance to show her concern for the missing men. Tehil was the first to hear it, a joyful sound carried on the wind. It was the song of return, and their song sent a message ahead of them—tonight they would eat their fill. The hunters entered the circle of their camp painted with the blood of a mare they had taken. Each of them carried a portion of the carcass equal in weight to their own. The horse was skinned at the killing site, and the rough, yellow hide, when dressed and stretched, would be big enough to make an entire wall of a tent. Naki's cousin, the joyful Zuya, wore the tail knotted through his own dark hair. It was his spear that struck the fatal blow and to him went the trophy of the kill. The people tittered with excitement. Their teeth clacked in anticipation and their mouths overflowed. The old ones rocked back and forth and hummed ancient prayers of thanks. A rumble of thanks went around the camp. *Nothing is Lost.* They dug a pit and built a huge bonfire as darkness approached. What they could not eat tonight would be salted and set on racks to dry for the days ahead.

For weeks, Sura was distracted by hunger. Now the anticipation of eating her fill gave her strength. The night was clear. She would read the sky, keep the vision in her head. Never be lost again. The Hunter, the ancestor of all the Huul, stood low in the sky, his spear aloft, shooting stars at celestial prey. And scattered among the limitless points of light that crowded the sky, the NesGras hearths she sought were few and far apart.

The people ate until their bellies ached, and then they ate some more. Sated and languid, they rose. Around and around the campfire they moved in a rhythmic stomping dance, giving thanks for their full stomachs. They struck the hooves together to mimic the sound of the galloping horse. Each of the hunters, in turn, told the story of the chase—how they tricked the horse into separating from the herd, how for two days it ran, until mad with thirst, fear, and exhaustion it faltered. The mare was the gold of the mountains, and its sweat was like the white foam of the sea.

They told the story again and again until it took on the measure of a song. They clattered and banged the long bones of the mare's forelegs and hammered the stretched skin with their strong hands until they could again hear the pounding hooves beating a desperate tattoo over the rocky land. They clapped their hands in time to the beating of their hearts. They drank the warm blood and savored the flesh, eating it raw, hunger overcoming the desire to make the meat tender over the fire. Babies with the tiniest of milk teeth were given slivers so that they would taste the spirit of the horse. All were intoxicated, heated by the fuel of abundant meat, the sharing of a glorious adventure, rapt by the sounds of thrumming sticks and bones, stretched hide, and voices that pushed away the fear of the dark.

The young girls moved from side to side, beating a countermeasure with their feet on the dancing ground. The young men stood and formed a circle closer to the leaping flames of the great central fire. The two groups danced in opposing concentric circles. Sura rose with the others, and like them, lost herself to the heat and the night. The fullness in her stomach suffused her senses. The camp was one pounding heart. Passing before her, as if in a dream, was Naki, whose face and body, while entirely familiar, was somehow completely different from the Naki of the day. His features transformed into the bold stare of the lion. He bristled with power, energy, and beauty. She was pulled toward him. His eyes fixed on her and hers on him. There was no one besides Sura and Naki in the pulsating shadows, and their blood sang an ancient song forever new. They did not touch, yet he filled her so that her skin was taut and would burst from the heat her flesh produced. Her feet moved, and she did not feel them touch the ground. She floated, but her body was so heavy, she needed to lie on the ground and pull Naki down with her. They sang the song of the dying horse, "Ay, ay. Ay, ay." The young men leapt high in the air chanting "Ay, ay," landing with shuddering force as their feet struck the ground. "Ay, ay." Children snorted and ran. "Ay, ay." They were horses, filled with the horse's flesh and galloping spirit. Sura started when she felt Tehil's hand slip into hers to pull her away from where she faced Naki. She looked away from him and saw the first rays of the sun erasing the shadow of the moon. The heat of the night evaporated from her skin. Alu stared at her with eyes the color of fire that burned without warmth.

Sura picked up her robe from where she had flung it when she joined the dance and wrapped it around herself. "I'm going outside to sleep," she said to Tehil. Many were beginning their daily routine despite the long night. Sura lay down among the long shadows. Somewhere east, past the high ring of mountains, was home. *Remember that*, she said to herself. She could hear the soft laughter of men and women lying together just beyond the outer circle of the campsite. She looked up at the cloudless sky, the infinite expanse of blue broken only by the solitary flight of a white sea bird. She pulled her robe around her. Only her face showed. It was cold and dry. The bright, clear winter sky held the hope of spring. She thought about the night. For the first time since she came to live with the Nir, she forgot to look at the stars. She offered no private prayer for Xur's life as she did every night since their separation. No thought of her father or brother intruded on the intense pleasure of watching Naki leap ahead of the flames, which seemed to struggle to reach him. *What have I lost?* she wondered. She explored her memory like a finger probing a wound, searching for the sharp grief that suffused her since Xur's fall. She felt the deep bond that was forming with Naki and with all the Nir. She tried to picture Xur and Bani, Esur and Mina resting around a fire, retelling the stories of their separation and pride, and of the NesGras, once many and now so few. One by one, she willed their images to appear. Naki's face, radiant in the flames' glow, rose to obliterate their memory. She closed her eyes against the light of day, yet, she saw him still; his face was the sun, red-hot, filling the entire sky. *No*, she thought, believing she was awake, *if I lose the memory of my family, then I will be truly lost.* "Bani," she said, "stay with me."

"Here I am, Sura," the voice of Bani whispered in her ear. When she turned to the voice, she saw the scrawny body of a whelp.

"Why are you so thin, Bani?" she asked.

"Because I would rather talk than suckle. Don't you remember?"

"I do," she said, as she took him into her arms and nursed him at her own breast.

She slept there on the still-frozen ground until midday. When she opened her eyes, her head ached from the light. She squeezed them shut and turned onto her side. Bursts of light flashed, then extinguished, across the miniature universe of her eyelids. The noon sun burned her nose, chin, and brow, creating warm spots on her otherwise cold skin. She was relieved that the sun resumed its normal size and had not set her on fire. She fixed her dreams in her memory even as the details faded away, stored against the day she would meet again with Mina, who would know more than the dreamer could.

The camp came to life. There was much to do. She rose slowly and stretched from the balls of her feet. She balanced on her toes, brown and round as chestnuts. Breathing deeply, Sura drew up from her waist, threw back her head, and extended her fingers toward the sky. Then she folded her sleeping robe, carefully rolled it up, and placed it inside the shelter. She gathered up her clothing. Sura slipped on her deerskin shift and wound it

twice around her body. She attached her blade and filled her pouch with
a chopper and some smooth, round stones for throwing. She flung a cape
of long-haired fox across her shoulders, smoothed her hair, picked up
her digging stick and spears, and just as she was about to leave, stuck a
feather—the lonely remnant of a past meal—behind her ear.

At the far end of the camp, Sura paused to watch Naki working a
piece of wood. His chin fit comfortably on his knees as he balanced on his
haunches. The muscles in his arms, the delicate strength in his wrists and
hands, and the sweet curve of his neck bent to his task pulled her toward
him. She needed to rouse herself from this strange state. She willed her feet
to walk away from him. *Where was I going?* It took her a minute to remember what she needed was in the high ground to the east. *That way.*

Naki considered the birch branch. Its diameter was the width of his
thumb. He pared away the bark. The wood beneath was smooth and dry
and pale. He cut the branch into small blanks nearly identical in size and
lay them on a square of coarse cloth pounded from the bark of the mother
tree. He shaped the blanks until they looked like little bones. When he
completed this step, he raised the pieces to his face and inhaled the warm,
sweet breath of the wood. Then he pressed them to his love-swollen heart,
imputing his spirit to the wood before placing them carefully back on the
cloth. He chose one and gripped it between the thumb and forefinger of his
left hand. With his right hand, he impressed a mark in the center with his
awl. He took the awl in his left hand, and keeping the point in the center of
the blank, he picked up his hammer stone and pierced the wood through
its center. Then he shaped it so that it would be as round and smooth as
Sura's flesh. He continued through the day, and when all the pieces of wood
were finished, he sat back and surveyed his handiwork with pleasure. Only
a few of the beads broke under the pressure of the stone. The rest looked up
at him, a row of unblinking eyes.

When he raised the beads to catch the scent once more, one fell and rolled in a narrowing spiral. Then it came to rest on its side. Naki dropped it again and again, taking pleasure in the bead's spiral dance.

Sura walked until she reached snow-covered higher ground. At midday, the stones sparkled. A light wind pushed through her nostrils and into her lungs. It was sweet and she swallowed it. The air massed and lifted her as she strode higher. The air surrounded her like a benign spirit sent by the sun to bring her happiness. She climbed higher, scaling boulders and stepping nimbly between the scattered rocks. The sun lowered in the sky. The wind stiffened and gave her strength. She paused to consider this propitious place. She cleared the sunlit area of all bits of growth and knelt and pressed her palms into the dirt. A pattern like outstretched wings was fixed on the ground. Sura stood and with her small spear struck it through its center and lifted her hands toward the source of the light.

"Mother," Sura said, "help us find our food today. Warn us when the beast is near. Comfort us when we feel pain. Smooth the path our spirits take."

She scooped a fistful of rocky soil from the ground. "*Nothing is lost,*" she said, as the wind spun the dirt around her.

Sura climbed higher. A shadow caught her eye and was gone. She stopped and flattened herself against the slope. The shadow panned slowly across the land. She looked up. The animal that glided only a small distance above her head was larger than any bird she had ever seen. It had thick, brown fur and a tail as long as its body. Its four legs were spread, and the membranes connecting them formed a furry cape. It came in to land on the cliff that jutted just over her head. Sura leapt and twisted with one swift movement. She grabbed the flying squirrel's tail, swung it to the ground, and knocked it on its head with her hammerstone. It let out a piercing squeal. For a flicker of a moment, she remembered that the cry was a herald of death, then she tucked the omen away from her thoughts and went back to the prayer site.

Sura slit the animal's throat and poured some of the blood onto the ground. She snipped a tuft of fur from its neck and tamped it down with the muddied blood. She withdrew her spear from the ground, wiped it, and replaced it in her quiver. An eagle asleep in its roost dreamt of the flesh of the woolly flying squirrel. On the ledge below, a hidden cave lion conspired with its mate to take the eagle while it slept. A hunter, confident in his strength, prepared an ambush as he rounded a distant hill on his way to the lion's lair. *Nothing is lost*, thought Sura as she returned to the camp to prepare her gift for Naki.

At daybreak, Sura disappeared to recover the pelt she had buried outside camp. She cleaned and scraped and pressed the fur, careful to keep the shape she saw glide over her head the afternoon before. When she finished, she raised the furry mantle and buried her face in its warm softness. Then she folded it gently and placed it inside her shift, next to her heart.

The camp was settling in for the night. Fires burned low. Children with full stomachs dozed as their parents told their history, remembered the faraway time, and shaped the story of yesterday's hunt to tell again and again. Sura entered the camp and walked toward the hearth that burned in the center. Naki rose and approached her. He held his gift in his hands.

"For you, Sura," he said.

He had strung the wooden beads on a plaited length of his own black hair. Sura took it from him. She inhaled its smoky wood and put it to her lips to taste its smoothness. It was sweet and salty at the same time. It stirred a hunger inside her.

"It is not food." Naki laughed. *It is*, thought Sura.

He placed it over Sura's head and it fell around her neck. The wood warmed her. She caressed each bead with her fingers. Their sweet breath matched her own. Without looking down, she could see her chest rising and falling as if she had run a great distance or was trapped a very long time underwater.

She reached into her shift and pulled out the flying squirrel mantle. She placed it on Naki's head and across his shoulders. His eyes gleamed so brightly that Sura thought she saw tears. His eyes shone so that neither Sura nor Naki noticed the glittering eyes of every other person in the camp fixed upon them.

Heavy rain halted the trek to the gathering of the Nir. Droplets of water rustled the branches of the shelter. After three days, they could find no dry kindling to feed the fires. Sura could see the small, gray heads of mice peeking from the corners where the walls skirted the ground. Rivulets of dusty water crept across the sloping floor. She blinked and the mice vanished. When she fell asleep, they would scurry across the dank floor to feed on the orts and crumbs of nuts and seeds and even dare to raid the dwindling sacks of food.

Everyone slept for most of the day and night curled into their bodies to conserve heat and energy. Why fight the mud and mold? Soon enough they would be on their way, and the sun would shine again. And if it did not, wasting energy on aimless pacing wouldn't persuade it to come back any sooner. In the gray twilight, the old fell into a reverie of hunts and great meetings of the past. The young had visions of adventures and feasts to come. All dreamed of the end of winter, of sweet sap flowing down the juniper tree, and living under a sun riding high in the sky.

"Alu!"

Sura, Tehil, and Zamia sprang upright at the shouted name.

"Alu!"

It was Manul's agitated voice coming from the entrance of the shelter. Alu opened her eyes at the sound and did not move. Manul burst in. The girls pressed against the side of the tent. It was forbidden for a man to enter the dwelling of a woman other than his wife, and Alu was no longer his wife. Alu looked at him without expression.

"Please help us," he said. His hair and clothing were disarrayed and soaked by the rain. "I beg you." The corners of Manul's mouth trembled in misery and humiliation.

Manul's young wife, Fox, was giving birth. Her sisters, inexperienced in childbirth, were in attendance. For ten hours she was in labor. Her water had broken, but the baby's head was not positioned in the birth channel. When they placed their hands on her stomach, they could feel the hard, round lump of his head high in the swell of her abdomen. He was so reluctant to enter this world that he had turned back within his mother's womb. There was only one person who could persuade the unborn soul to life, and that was the person who made an offering in the woods to the spirits of destruction. The evil cairn that Alu built worked its magic and would destroy Manul and his little family starting now with the baby, and swiftly thereafter, his young mother.

Manul dug his fists into his eyes and, without warning, threw himself at Alu's feet. Sura, Tehil, and Zamia looked on in astonishment. Alu slowly rose and looked down at Manul's prostrated body with no more concern than if he were a beetle caught in her grain sack. Sura was certain that Alu was going to put her foot on the back of Manul's head and crush his face into the dirt floor.

"Help us, Alu, and the child shall be yours."

Alu's face angled into a smile. "Mine?" The possibilities of a child at her old age, robbed from her enemies, intrigued her.

"Get up, Manul. I will come."

Alu took her medicine pouch from a branch, and as leisurely as if she was taking a stroll to look for turnips, walked to the far end of the camp where the moans of Fox weighed heavily on the rank air.

All eyes in the camp focused on Alu as she neared the shelter. Alu entered and looked at the breaching girl. The baby's feet were protruding from her body. Fox's sisters were by turns screaming and pulling their hair, then grabbing the little feet, now purple and waxen despite, or because of, their useless efforts. Alu kneeled at Fox's feet and pushed the girl's legs so that they were bent at the knees, shifting her strength to the center of her body where she could ride the contractions. She placed one hand under Fox's buttocks and with the other gently stroked her stomach. "Breathe," she whispered, "breathe for the child." She directed Fox's sisters to make a decoction of the herbs she had taken with her and to give Fox little sips of the liquid to quench her thirst. Alu stroked and kneaded Fox's stomach. She rubbed her all over with aromatic oils and cooled her brow with water. When the fire burned low, she said to Manul, "Fool, tend the fire," never taking her eyes from the suffering girl.

"Fuel for the fire, yes, Alu," said Manul, unfolding himself from the corner to feed the dying embers. Fox's moans turned to shrieks that vibrated the ground on which she thrashed, and twigs and dirt woven into the shelter roof rained down on the sisters who now hugged each other and whimpered. Manul threw sticks on the fire and strained to glimpse at Fox. All the while, Alu kneaded the girl's stomach, whispering as if she did not hear the cries of pain.

Alu watched her, stroked her, and urged her on gently to push the legs, then the body, of the baby into her waiting hands. When the little boy's chest emerged, Alu gently lifted and rotated him until his mouth and nose began to emerge. Then with one swift movement, he was clear of his mother's body. Alu's deft fingers unwrapped the cord that was wound around his neck and sucked the mucous from his nose and mouth. With her left hand cradling the small body, she pinched the tiny nose and breathed into the slack, little mouth. She rubbed the baby's chest and felt for a sign of a living heart, then she blew her breath once more into the still lungs. The baby's legs hung limply on either side of her cradling wrist; her fingers steadied the lolling head. Alu bent to his mouth once more and breathed into his. All at once, the baby's piercing cries filled the camp. Manul, mindful of his promise, said, "You have a son, Alu."

She looked at him, then turned to the sisters who were waiting for her instructions.

"Clean him," she said. "Put him to her breast. Call me when the cord stops pulsing."

She left at the same pace as she had come, and as she walked, she could be heard trying out names for her new son: *Lion of Alu, Magic of Alu, Gift of Alu.* She would take her time to come up with a name that would honor her in the way she felt she deserved.

She had carried nine children and three survived—Naki, Dzo, and Tehil. *If I could have worked my birthing magic on myself,* she thought, *they all would have lived.* Alu, the youngest daughter of the great healer, Tell, knew so much. She had the gift. In her memory, seasons, births and deaths, plant lore, and magic all came together to produce one powerful core. Her children, however, were like Manul, content in the joy of the moment, careless of the knowledge she tried to pass on to them. *No,* thought Alu, *it is a stranger who has the ability to learn the secrets of the natural world and of the world beyond.*

CHAPTER EIGHT

NIGHT SKY

Xur's strength and stamina increased as the days grew longer. At night he studied the sky, and by day, he worked bone and leather, stone and wood. He showed the children how to make tools, clothing, and shelter from the raw landscape. Esur listened to his son retell the ancient narrative and remembered the boy he once was, enthralled by the visions conjured around the campfire of his parents. He drifted to sleep as Xur's voice, higher in range than his, cadenced like his Willow mother's, lulled them with intimations of what lie beyond the observed world. How else could they shine light on the unseen forces that propelled it? What was time except the recurring cycles of days and months and seasons, an eternal spiral with no beginning and no end? The stories connected the small bands of the Huul with each other. Wherever they traveled, they encountered people who shared the awe of the unforgiving natural world and the boundary of their existence.

What were the glittering stars that got no closer no matter how high they climbed, that moved as they did with the seasons? The stars were hearths, they said, for the spirits of those who left their bodies in the dust of the earth, in the bat-besmirched caves, or in the frozen waters of winter. Why on a clear night could they see so many? There was no word for this abundance, no satisfaction for their infinite curiosity. Their only recourse was to break down the vastness of the night sky into discrete images that they could understand and explain: a bear and her cubs, a hunter with a raised spear, hearths for ancestors beyond living memory. Look up, the storytellers invited; the night sky knows all secrets.

Xur and Bani were awake under the canopy of light against black, a bearskin blanket stretched between them and the frost-covered ground.

"Where is the Hunter?" asked Bani, his dark eyes mirroring the lights above.

"There," said Xur, tracing the starry outline with his finger.

"And where is his brother?" asked Bani.

"No, Bani," said Xur, "the wolf that walks behind him is not his brother. He is his father. In the time before the Hunter, the people were beasts. They walked as all beasts do on four legs. Their snouts were close to the ground. They called to each other with howls and barks. They did not make weapons because they had claws and teeth as sharp as blades and jaws stronger than the grip of any man."

"I have never seen a wolf," said Bani.

"That is because the wolf can smell you and hear you from far away, before you can get close to him. He is so fast that if you did get near him, you would think only that a puff of wind had passed. He hunts with such cunning that he becomes one with his band. Even the bear, with all of his strength and ferocity, is brought down."

"If the wolf is all those things, why did he make his son a man?"

"Because the wolf," said Xur, "could not do the one thing he desired most. So he traded his warm fur and sharp teeth and claws so that he could rise up from the ground and speak."

Bani drew his hand from under his cover and examined it in the near darkness. He traced his fingers over his face and across his soft mouth.

"Do you think it was a good trade?" asked Xur.

Bani was silent, and Xur thought he was asleep. As Xur nestled down under the heavy furs, Bani replied, "I think you would have to ask the wolf."

After a moment, he said, "Tell me the story, Xur."

The hunter and his son chased the rabbit to the region where the forest meets the desert. The hunter stopped to rest, and the younger wolf, who had not yet learned restraint, ran on despite the warning his father sent him on the wind. The rabbit vanished into the gullies and shadows of the forest. The son of the wolf, filled with the joy of speed, could not stop.

The iridescent wings of a raven fluttered in and out among the trees. She was bright and black by turns, lit by the sun, then lost in the shade, then sparkling like water flowing through the sun's rays. The bird seemed to beckon the wolf to follow, but when he reached the center of an assembly of oaks, he became confused and spun foolishly, looking for the direction she had taken.

A voice from a branch high over his head sang, "Tell me your name."

He looked up as the bird fanned her wings against the bright sky, blurring the outline of her feathers. He tried to sing his name to her in tones that would express what was in his heart. Instead, a baleful howl caught in his throat. He reared up on his hind legs to reach the branches where she perched, and he lost his balance and fell against the rough trunk. His very nature was routed by the desire to declare himself to her, and he cursed his clumsy limbs and inarticulate mouth for failing him. Words of endearment emerged as snarls, and his mordant teeth bit his beastly tongue till blood ran down his throat.

The spirit of the oak was roused by the wolf's unhappiness and took pity on him. First, he stripped the wolf of his soft and luxuriant fur. The wolf stood naked, exposed to the ridicule of all the other beasts. Still, he reached for the raven. Then the spirit shaped the wolf's mouth until it was as tender and harmless as a suckling cub's. He molded the wolf's claws into a shape that could hold whatever he could reach, but he left the throbbing heart of the wolf

unchanged as he transformed him into the thing we call a man. The man
embraced the raven as his wife, and her raven locks and lissome voice keep
him, to this very day, enthralled.

Xur closed his eyes and folded his hands across his stomach as if to
say, The End.

"Wait," said Bani. "Does that mean that we have the heart of a wolf?"

"Is that what you think it means?" asked Xur.

"I don't know what it means." He waited for Xur to tell him, but Xur
said nothing.

"Xur, if we have the same heart as the wolf, does that make us good
or bad?"

"Why do you ask that, Bani?"

"Nin said that the wolf kills for pleasure, for the pride in his skill, not
only because he is hungry."

"Some have said so," said Xur.

"Nin said that the wolf kills the weak and the old and fears the hooves
and antlers of the stag."

"Does Nin not fear the hooves and antlers of the stag?"

"Nin says that the wolf hunts like a coward. He bites the elk from
behind because he's afraid of him."

"Brother, don't judge the wolf differently than you would judge a
man whose heart beats with cowardly fear and runs from the beast without
throwing his spear. The same heart, whether a man's or a wolf's, can face
the worst danger. I mean to say, Bani, that sometimes we are all afraid."

"So," said Bani, "sometimes the wolf is good and brave, and sometimes he is bad and cowardly."

Xur nodded.

"When Nin wakes up tomorrow, I'll tell him it's not bad to be afraid."

"Bani," said Xur, "the story of the wolf—it's not only about bravery."

"I know." Bani yawned.

"It's about the pull of the heart when one confronts the other."

"The other what?" asked Bani as his eyes closed.

"The other sex," said Xur.

Bani could measure the cycles of the moon to track the seasons. He could calculate the length of a day's journey by the position of the sun.

Bani could measure the cycles of the moon to track the seasons. He could calculate the length of a day's journey by the position of the sun. From Mina, he learned to use plants for food and medicine. He learned the meanings of the signs painted on the rocks and impressed in the earth. He learned to dream and to bring the knowledge that he learned in his dreams to the others. He never forgot a story, yet never tired of hearing stories retold.

Mina would say, "Mother's spirit dwells with his. He is a child with two souls."

Bani spent the morning gathering chert and flint. "Bring back stones the size of my fist," Xur said to him. Bani went off toward the valley between two mountains with a hammerstone and the directions to test the worthiness of the stone.

"Hammer off a chip. If it is smooth, the flake will be sharp and the core strong," said Xur.

Bani removed his leather apron, tied it over his shoulders to form a sack, and filled it with the carefully chosen stones. He went back to camp, proud to show Xur the bounty of his efforts.

"What is this, Bani?" asked Xur, holding up a pink, egg-shaped stone.

"Quartz," said Bani.

"And this?" asked Xur.

Bani studied the deep-red stone. "Jasper," he said.

Xur and Bani sat on either side of a wide, gray rock that looked like a tree stump that had turned to stone. Xur put a black rock on its flat surface. On its tight, vertical ridges, the rock reflected the afternoon light like moonlight on water.

"When did you get that, Xur?"

"I got this, Bani, when you were gathering leaves for Mina's tea. Can you name it?"

Every animal, every plant, every stone had a name. Without a name, they would disappear from the world and return to a blind place, a huge, black, infinite maw colder than winter's wind. Bani shuddered. He did not know the name.

"It is obsidian, the stone that makes the sharpest blades."

Obsidian. Bani rolled the word soundlessly in his mouth. *Obsidian.*

"First, we will take this red stone . . ." Xur paused.

"Jasper," said Bani.

". . . and we will make a hammer."

Xur held the oval stone in his left hand and a hammerstone in his right, and with a short, quick snap of his wrist and forearm, he broke the oval in half.

"Now you," he said to Bani.

Bani took the heavy hammerstone from Xur and another piece of jasper from the stack of rocks beside them. His hands were half as big as Xur's and shook with the effort of keeping a firm grip. He steadied the rock on the stone slab that was used as an anvil. With his right arm, he swung the hammerstone in a wide arc toward the oval of the jasper. To his amazement, he missed his target completely.

"Good," said Xur, ignoring Bani's disappointment. "Do it again. This time, don't swing your arm, just hit straight down."

Bani swung, missed, and swung again, but never managed so much as a chip. Xur knelt behind him and put his big hands over Bani's.

"Think of the anvil, not the rock. The anvil waits for your hands to learn."

Each day, the sun stayed in the sky longer. The freezing rains of winter bit less deeply and less often. The time for the Great Meeting was drawing near. They would follow the star that held fast in the great, circular center of the sky. The tracks of the NesGras, the Willow, the Wolf Moon, and the Nir would meet at Huul, the Cave of the Goats.

Bani knew that when the time came, the moon would be showing half of her face. He tracked the moon's cycle of change, marking a shaft of wood each night with a small, curved line. For a long time, he puzzled over how to depict the nights when the moon completely hid her face, finally settling upon a single stroke of his burin. For the nights of the full moon, he carved the curved lines close together, facing each other to resemble the full, round face of the moon. There were few who could limn that recurring image. They were chosen by their inclination to curiosity, tenacity, and the great gift of memory. They searched the shifting sky for patterns and probed the traveling fires that smoldered far above their heads. Bani's hands and eyes seemed to be aligned by an imaginary string: he looked and what he saw flowed from his hands to the wood so that what he saw others could see also. Tell, the fearsome Eagle of Mina's stories, could read the sky. Tell knew when it was time to hunt, time to fish, and time to choose hunger and dream. However much Bani missed his sister, he longed even more to sit at Tell's campfire and see what the old man saw.

CHAPTER NINE

THE BEAR

The NesGras men, Rosh, Ququr, Xur, and the boys, Nin and Bani, descended in a single file behind Esur. They reached a sloping plateau at the end of a narrow pass where tiny, green buds were evidence of winter-spared life. They agreed it was a good place to meet. Foreshortened shadows under the noon sun gave them time to look for food and still get back to their home camp before dark. They broke into two groups to cover more ground and to separate the boys. "Too much talk," said Esur, who put his big hand on Bani's shoulder and steered him in front. Bani winked at Nin, who frowned back, then hurried to catch up to his own father.

Winter was retreating. The season of wakefulness, of early sunrise and late sunset, was coming in its time. Day and night were in accord. Xur could almost forget the ache in his leg and shoulder. The sun healed and conferred strength and comfort to everyone. The sun moved by day and slept by night as they did, chasing the winter gloom. Xur felt a surge of hope. His father, who not so long before reminded him of a solid block in his youthful path, now inspired his regard. Bani, the living link to his mother, walked alongside him. When Bani forgot his father's rebuke, he clamped his hand over his mouth and rolled his eyes to signal Xur that he knew not to break the hunters' silence. For the first time since he was separated from Sura, Xur felt joy. The sun was a powerful presence. Under its protection, what unhappy star could cause them further harm?

They all grew lean during the winter. Ququr's big nose looked bigger in his wide face. Long before Nin was born, when Mina's unfriendly Willow relatives asked why that ugly NesGras man was always smiling, she answered them with her own smile.

Ququr, Rosh, and Nin were the first to return to the plateau with their cache: two squirrels, two wood rats, a mole they dug up that appeared dead when they found it but was just slow to wake, three duck eggs, green-stemmed onions with their long roots dangling, and a treat for the children to share later—a sweet, yellow honeycomb. The shadows grew longer, and they anticipated the trip back to camp with Esur and his sons. They were hungry and built a small fire, quickly skinned the squirrels, skewered them with their digging sticks, and began to roast them along with the pungent onion. The afternoon wind picked up and blew the flavors of their meal to their companions, who hurried to meet them. And the wind also signaled their presence to a hungry creature waking after a long sleep.

Her snout moved like a probing finger in the air. Roasting meat, onions, eggs, and honey, strong enough to disguise the repellant odor of man. Her body fat depleted, her massive bones weakened, her muscles ached for sustenance. Two wobbly cubs followed close behind her. Her brown coat of matted fur swung loosely as she propelled toward the scent of food. Nin, not seeing or even suspecting that he stood on the course the bear had set, skipped stones across the path where he expected Bani and the others to appear.

Without breaking her pace or growling a warning, she was in the clearing, charging directly toward Nin. Ququr was about to call Nin to warn him not to go off by himself when he saw the bear. He leaped past the fire and ran in front of his startled son. With one swipe of her powerful claws, the bear flung Ququr to the ground. The boy screamed in terror, drawing the bear's attention away from his father. Ququr grabbed his digging stick as the bear turned on Nin again. She ran sideways, her fur cresting, displaying her great size. She growled and snapped her jaws, driven to frenzy now that her prey was fighting back. Ququr aimed for her left eye and plunged the sharpened end in through the socket as the bear held him to the ground and with her front paws on his chest, tore at his scalp.

Xur, Esur, and Bani, alarmed by the boy's terrible screams, ran to the camp as the wounded bear flipped Ququr over, dragged him across the ground, and bit into his flesh. Rosh, Esur, and Xur plunged their spears into the back and ribs of the bear. She reared, taller than any of the men, infuriated by the onslaught of pain. She twisted, looking for her cubs. Xur smashed a rock against her skull and she toppled. One last foul breath was expelled and she was still.

Nin did not move. His mouth was open, as if he was screaming, but there was only silence.

"They have killed each other." Bani began to sob.

Esur put his ear to Ququr's chest. "Not yet, Bani."

The bear's saliva, along with the dirt that covered them both, would poison Ququr's wounds. His only chance for survival was to somehow clean the lacerations and find a way to close them before infection set in. Gashes striped his chest. Flesh was torn from the back of his thigh. His skull was exposed where his scalp was ripped. They were far from a source of fresh water and the sun was setting. They were completely exposed to the elements and to other predators, who, unlike the bear, hunted at night, in packs, and could smell the blood-steeped camp from miles away.

Esur ran his hand along Ququr's spine. He gently rolled him onto his side and placed a robe between his body and the ground. Putting his fingers in Ququr's mouth to make sure his tongue did not slip down his throat, he raised his head so he wouldn't choke on his own blood and vomit. Bani built the fire. Ququr must not be allowed to freeze, and he needed the light to tend him. Xur, pain from his own recent wounds put aside, ran with great speed toward the last place he had seen water. Nin held his father's hand while Esur tore Ququr's clothing into strips. He cleaned the blood from Ququr's face and head and searched for wounds made by the bear's sharp canine teeth. The heavy bleeding, frightening to look at, washed the wound and kept his skin from drying out. Esur had to decide quickly. Should he close the tear in Ququr's scalp and risk a slow, agonizing death from infection, or wait for Xur to return with the water to pour into the wound and risk imminent death from loss of blood. He let it bleed and turned to the thigh wound. He carefully cleaned it, throwing the mucous and blood-soaked strips into the fire as he did. The chest lacerations would have to wait.

Bani gathered dry grass and kindling from the bushes that ringed the plateau and built a fire. He placed rocks in a ring around the fire to heat. He positioned the rocks next to Ququr's body when they grew warm and exchanged them when they cooled down. He rolled pieces of hide into padding to keep Ququr from rolling onto his back while Esur worked on his wounds.

Xur ran toward the light of Bani's fire, clutching two bladders filled with water. Esur carefully lifted Ququr's head and trickled some water between his lips. Xur poured a thin stream of water over his scalp, while Esur quickly laid the flap of flesh and hair over the skull. From his kit, he took a ball of tree gum and secured the torn edges of flesh with small, flattened pieces he rolled and softened between his thumb and forefinger. He watered the thigh wound and wrapped cloth that he had scorched in the flames loosely around it. Last, he cleaned and covered the chest lacerations.

Rosh and Xur skinned the bear and called to Bani to help them butcher the meat. They could take no more than the boys could carry back to camp. The rest would be left for the scavengers that were gathering in the shadows. Rosh, Esur, and Xur would carry Ququr back, taking turns at the handles of the litter, their backs weighted with tools and weapons, vulnerable now that their strongest member was down.

Ququr's hands and feet were cold despite the fire and the clothing the others had taken off to cover him. Nin still held his father's hand, letting go only to exchange the stones for warm ones. Ququr's face was swollen, and the bruises were turning from deep red to black. His scalp, in spite of Esur's best efforts, sat askew on his skull. "Breathe, Father," Nin whispered. He put his head to Ququr's chest. His heart's uncertain rhythm seemed to stop then start again. Ququr needed Mina's herbs and her invocations. He needed the fresh water that flowed near the campsite. He needed all of the members of his family to survive.

Xur called to his father. Esur walked to where Xur labored, separating the bear's dense flesh from her thick hide. With his blade, he trimmed the hide to form a shape that could cradle Ququr's body. Folds of fur from the bear's limbs would be placed under Ququr's head, back, and knees to cushion against the unavoidable rolling and bumping of their gait as they walked over the uneven landscape. They bored holes on the long sides of the pelt. Two thick digging sticks were pushed through the holes long enough to extend as handles. They tied them in place and padded the ends where they would grasp the litter for the long trip back.

Rosh and Xur heaved the pelt above the fire to dry and to purge it of vermin. The hard odor of blood was a tale that all of the creatures—scavengers, predators, or prey—could perceive on the wind.

Bani's tears fell on the flesh of the bear, sweet still, as he separated muscle from bone and the claws from the appendages that left a mark on the earth like a giant human hand. No hint of life remained in them, so powerful only a few hours before. The bear's head, too big for him to lift, one small, black eye obliterated, the other sunken and opaque, transfixed him with terror. Where was the bear's spirit? Was it trapped in the mangled body of Ququr, struggling still to rip his life away? Bani could hear the cubs cry for their mother. It was for them that the bear rushed into their camp, to take the food so that they would live. It was for Nin that Ququr killed the bear, had, in fact, killed himself by stepping between them.

Xur took the meat from Bani's hands and completed preparing the bundles that he and Nin would carry. Bani's eyes fluttered in exhaustion, and he tottered over onto his side and slept. Nin, still clutching his father's hand, fought to stay awake until at last he, too, fell asleep.

Esur and Xur aligned the bearskin, fur to the ground, next to Ququr's body. They lifted him onto the litter. Esur and Xur took their positions, front and back, and called to Bani and Nin to rise in the predawn darkness and pick up their bundles. Rosh carried everything else. They did not utter a sound until the sun rose, and they bowed their heads and thanked the sun for rising.

The men changed positions from time to time. The man in front had to hold the handles awkwardly behind his back to protect Ququr's head from bouncing. On steep inclines, Rosh braced Ququr's body, holding him steady to avoid pressing into his wounds. Whenever they passed the still partially frozen streams, they gathered ice. As it thawed, they gave water to Ququr, then drank themselves, sweating under their clothes despite the cold. They moved in tandem and changed positions often, sharing and conserving as much of their strength as they could.

They arrived at camp as the sun withdrew its warmth. Mina, pacing the outer rim of the campsite, gasped when she saw them approach. She quickly suppressed her alarm and ran to them. First, she took the bundles from Bani and Nin and alerted the others in the camp. Then she raced back to the men and grasped the handles that Esur had been holding. She walked backward, facing Xur, toward the overhang of rock they used for shelter. Xur's muscles were taut, his veins swollen and visibly throbbing.

Rosh set down his burden of food, tools, and weapons and relieved Xur of his end of the litter. Xur's fingers curled from the long hours of gripping. He stumbled beneath the shelter where Esur and the boys had already lain down and fell asleep.

Ququr moaned without cease in a voice that was neither human nor animal. His spirit was caught in a place of unutterable horror, and the unconnected words that tumbled out along with his screams gave no sign of the place he had gone.

Mina tended her husband as she had done Xur. She soothed him with words that once delighted him, fed him liquids, cleaned him, and kept him warm. Then she prayed and performed all the rituals she knew to nourish his spirit. Still, he moaned. The whole camp succumbed to despair. A cold rain fell. The biting wind and the voice of constant pain ate at their souls. Esur's neck and fingers were held in a wrenching grip that no amount of willow tea could relax. Xur stared bleary-eyed at the puddles and pressed his palms into the dull ache in his temples. The children did not play games. Their eyes took on a listless stare, and their voices fell to whispers. The group could not move on and leave Ququr behind to die like a rabid animal, yet by staying on too long, they would deplete the resources of this bleak place. The time of the gathering of the Huul was approaching—a time they missed for too many years. For life's sake, they needed the reciprocation of companionship and experiences. They needed the exchange of things that they shaped, wore, and ate. They needed the infusion that a mingling of their bloodlines would bring.

Mina left Ququr's side and went into the forest. When she returned late in the day, her pouch was filled with a plant whose withered, purplish stalks were as long as she was tall. Some new sprouts grew from the large root, and these Mina broke off and gave to the children. When Nin reached out to touch the gnarly root, Mina rebuked him with uncharacteristic harshness.

She ground the root along with some long, black seeds that clung to the dry stalks. She placed the stalks in a vessel filled with water and set it aside. As the others slept, Mina worked through the night preparing two mixtures. When she was finished, she took the tincture prepared from the roots and seeds and pressed it between Ququr's lips. When the dose was complete, she took the remainder to the edge of the forest and flung it away. She took a sip of the second mixture, and soon her eyes grew heavy and she fell asleep.

The next morning, Xur was the first to wake. He became aware of the silence and rushed to Ququr, expecting that he had died in the night. But Ququr opened his eyes and smiled up into Xur's surprised face. Xur roused the rest, and they all gathered around him. All that day, Ququr was at ease. He responded to the children's touches and to Mina's voice. He whispered into Nin's ear and Nin nodded. He looked around and seemed assured that he rested within the circle of his people. Before night fell again, he closed his eyes, his smile slipped away, and he slept without stirring.

Mina sheared her long braid and folded Ququr's hand around it. They buried him in a robe made from the litter that carried him back for the last time. His favorite tools were laid beside his flexed body, along with a shaft he had started to shape into a spear. They worked throughout the day to cover his body with rocks and dirt. The next morning, they started again on their march north to the Great Meeting.

Nin never repeated what his father whispered in his ear that day. "The bear," Ququr said, "told me that she knows now that you meant no harm to her cubs, and she would like you to forgive her."

CHAPTER TEN

WINTER

Zamia and Tehil went with Sura as far as their grandfather's tent and pushed her toward the entrance. A voice called her in. Sura lifted a corner of the flap and stepped inside.

She had never seen a shelter as large as this. Her whole family could lie down inside without touching shoulders. Walls of hide stretched over a framework of poles nearly twice her height. The back wall was the exterior of the mountain, straight except for shadowed niches. A low fire in the center of the tent gave off just enough light to see into the corners. A cutout of sky showed through an opening at the top where white smoke spiraled and dispersed. Inside, a mantle of haze lingered, making everything soft-edged and dreamlike. Vessels of various sizes, skins from small animals, wooden items whose purpose she did not know, hung from the frame. As her eyes adjusted to the dark, she saw a bundle of hides stacked in one corner of the shelter along with stone axes and firewood. Tell stood opposite her across the fire. He was short, even by Nir standards, with nothing between his wrinkled skin and angled bones. Around his waist, his upper arms, and below his knees, he wore strips of hide decorated with feathers and shells. A rack of antlers appeared to grow out of his skull, which spouted random wisps of white hair. When Sura got up the nerve to glance at his face, it seemed cooked, a layer of desiccated flesh stretched over burnt bone. *Alu's father, Tell,* she thought, spoken of with deep respect around the campfire: *The Old One.*

"So you are Sura," he said.

She tried not to stare at his nose. Thin as a blade, its curved tip pointed to the spot in his beard where his mouth was hidden. He tilted his head back to look down at her, although she was taller than him, even with his antlers.

"And what is your father's name?"

"Esur."

"Your brother's?"

"Xur and—"

"So, you all share the same name, a NesGras peculiarity," he said to the air.

She started to protest that their names were really quite different. He nodded, his antlers arcing in agreement with his own observation.

"And what is your age?"

She held one finger up for the winter that passed since she was counted as an adult.

"Good," he said, "at least you know that."

He noticed the finely made quartz blade secured at her waist. He gestured toward it, and Sura handed it to him. He examined the tool, carved by Xur and given to her the year before. Each pink facet reflected the fire in a blade so delicate, it appeared to be cut from water. Someone, hidden until now in the shadows, moved close to Tell's left side to get a better look at the blade. From the shape of her face, the sharp nose, the luminous eyes, except for her smile, she could be Alu's twin.

"It is well made," he said, balancing the blade on his flattened palm. He turned to his daughter, or was it his wife (Sura was not sure) and whispered, "The NesGras make beautiful yet useless tools."

Sura flushed at the insult to Xur's hand. *It has been used many times,* she thought, ashamed that she did not dare speak the words aloud. He gave the blade back to her as Alu entered the shelter and took her place at the right side of her father. They studied her like vultures around a carcass.

Sura became aware of her hands. They were on her hips—an untoward sign of defiance. She let them hang limply at her sides, then held them at her back, then folded her arms across her chest, finally deciding to clasp them behind her. The flames licked at Sura's cheeks. *How strange that such a small fire could produce so much heat,* she thought. She needed air, yet her feet, stuck to the smooth dirt floor, ignored her pleas to carry her outside.

At last Tell said, "You were wrong to leave your brother, even if you meant to help him."

Sura was stung. It was true. She was wrong to leave Xur.

"You are a very bold girl to travel so far with strangers. Somehow the spirits favored you," he said, sweeping his arm grandly before him, "by bringing you here."

"Thank you," said Sura, not feeling favored at all.

"Oho," said Tell, "she knows some manners." His smiling daughter (wife?) laughed as Alu narrowed her eyes and jerked her head in annoyance.

"It is said that you and Naki have looked at each other. Is this true?"

Sura wished the fire would turn her to ash.

"And that you have exchanged gifts?"

"Yes," she said, wondering if all of her thoughts were as easily read as her feelings for Naki. Sura's hand went to the beads that circled her bare neck.

"I was grateful when. . . ." Before she could finish, Alu waved her away without looking at her, and the three turned their backs and began to talk to each other. Sura found her feet and fled through the flap to the waiting girls who almost had their ears pressed to the outside of the tent. They pumped her arms up and down, laughed, and begged her to tell them what was said.

"Did he mention Naki? Did Naki ask for you to stay with us and be a Nir? Did you tell him that you wish to stay with us? What did our mother, Alu, say?"

"She said nothing." Tell's words continued to echo in her mind. The old man knew everything. Sura's foolish decision to leave Xur and travel the unknown distance home was arrogance. By now, everyone knew that Sura's brother was found. Just days before, two men passing through the Nir camp carried rumors of a young man who was left to die by his companion. Errant travelers—sometimes solitary, sometimes in groups of two or three young men—were always welcomed and fed by the settled groups. In exchange, they carried news from one part of the far-flung Huul to another.

"Was he alive?" Sura asked them.

They believed he was, they answered.

"Did you see him?"

"Not I," said one, "but my cousin did."

"Did he look like me?" asked Sura.

"No," the second man said, "he looked like a man."

"I mean, did he look like a NesGras man?"

"Oho," said the first man, as if stunned by a new insight before his face turned thoughtful.

"The people in the NesGras camp looked very much like you."

"See," said Tehil, "just as I said. Your brother is well, and you are, too."

Sura wanted to ask them more, as the others crowded in around them. They had brothers and sisters, and mothers and fathers who were far away and wanted to hear news of them.

Forgive me, Xur, she thought. *Forgive me.*

That day, they held the celebration for the new son of Alu. He was called Mag, *he who is a gift to his mother,* an ancient name among the Nir. Fox nursed the baby, but it was Alu who held him when his finger was pricked with a thorn and the drops of blood were offered to the earth. The baby howled, and they all laughed as if the baby's cries were hilarious. All except Manul and Fox, who stood off to one side with stricken smiles on their faces. The number of people assembled on this hilltop awed Sura. She had not seen so many living creatures together since a band of horses had thundered near her home camp. And these were only the nearby bands of the Nir. Except for the noise, she was growing accustomed to the tumultuous assemblage of celebrating people. What would her family think of this gathering? Fires burned everywhere at once. Shelters were large enough to hold so many of Tehil's cousins that Sura lost track of their names. By the end of the day, all the young women blurred into one featureless face that vaguely resembled Tehil.

Zamia's and Tehil's warm arms touched hers on either side. Naki walked with his mother and grandfather and turned often to smile at her across the crowd. All this time, she prayed to return to her people and see for herself if Xur left that ledge on his feet or in the belly of a lion. Many nights, the intensity of her tears roused her from sleep, and the dreams of her family's embrace dissolved in the darkness. She needed Mina to explain why leaving the Nir made her heart ache, and why it ached even more at the thought of leaving her family. She knew that once a woman took her place in her husband's clan, there was no promise that she would ever see her own family again. She hated her fears. All of the encouragement and affection that Tehil and Zamia fed her would end when they left the Nir to be part of their own husbands' clans. There was no other way. Alu managed the feat against all custom by marrying Manul, the most ordinary of men and a blood relative. But Alu was no ordinary woman. Women could choose their mates, and Alu chose to stay within the clan of her father, Tell, the eagle of the Huul.

It would be some time before Sura and Naki could be alone together. The seasons would repeat themselves at least once before that could happen. Until then, she and Naki made a tacit promise to only look on each other. She had no experience in courtship. Esur did not take another wife after her mother died. Xur had not yet chosen a mate from the Willow or the Wolf Moon, and certainly not from the Nir. Until now, the NesGras and the Nir avoided each other. It was rarely discussed why. In the meantime, her friends did everything they could to ease her loneliness, and Sura believed that with the exception of Alu, the Nir were the gentlest and most generous of people.

Tehil said, "What is one winter, Sura? It is like a night of restless sleep. The sun rises, and the torments of cold and wind are forgotten. You look doubtful, but you will see soon enough. Travelers will tell your family that in the season of the thrush, all the clans of Huul will journey east, away from the great sea and over the hills. We will gather on the shore of the sweet water lake. The rain will overflow the ring of land and bring the grains and grasses that welcome the warm season. Fish and birds and small animals will be trapped in our nets. Deer and goats will present their young to join us in our feast. Can you taste it? No drowning. No hunger. No fear."

While Tehil spun a story of gentle weather and abundance, Sura thought of ice and frozen lakes, of small birds devouring the berries on their rush south, of hawks and black vultures, first to find the dead, that would eat the prey they shared with humans and leave only the bones for hyenas. Bears, enraged that the fish still slumbered beneath the frozen waters, would lose their fat. Blind, long-haired rhinos would run the weakest of us down. And the strong would eat dirt to survive.

"Eat dirt? What are you talking about, Sura?"

Sura looked up. The quail had started its migration along the eastern shore.

"See," Tehil said, "when we are all together, the quail will meet us and be guests at the great feast."

"Yesterday, I saw an ibex," said Zamia, trying to distract Sura.

"Was it a male or a female?" asked Tehil with a little too much enthusiasm.

"A male, and his horns spanned the space between two canyon walls, which he climbed by leaping like this." And Zamia leaped from one foot to another to show how the ibex caught the shallow crevices with pointed hooves, rising like a leaf on a current of air.

"I wish I saw that, don't you, Sura?" asked Tehil.

"I was wrong to leave my brother."

"Sura, we promise, after the winter, you will see him and your family. Just as surely as the quail follows the sun, you will see them again."

Afterward, Sura remembered a story that Mina told her when she was a small child. It was from the time when the four clans of the Huul were united: the Willow from the north, the Nir from the west, the Wolf Moon from the south, and the NesGras from the east.

"We rode in on the wind, and the sun winked at us and assured us that we were not abandoned. But as punishment for wrongs we had no memory of committing, the wind began to regard us as beings of no consequence. It quenched our fires. We took shelter in the caves and it followed us. When we left to look for food, the wind blew our coverings into the treetops and left us naked. It tossed us like leaves across the frozen ground. The wind was so cold, it stoppered our breath with ice. It took all air from us to feed its own greed. What could grow when the wind is so angry? The very young and the very old could not suck life from the whirlwind that paused outside our campsites only to gather force and take us by surprise."

"Did everyone die, Mother?" asked Sura.

"No, the young and the strong lived, but with no grandfather or grandmother to teach them, no children to make them laugh and bring them hope, they suffered not only the corporal punishment of the wind, but loneliness and dread tore at their spirits as well. And so it continued, season after season, until the clans were scattered across the land, each blaming the other for the wrongs committed against the wind."

Sura interrupted again. "Were you there, too, Mina?"

Xur snickered. "She just said it was in Grandfather's time."

"No, Sura, my mother's father was still a small Willow child who had to be lashed to a tree trunk to keep him from joining the skyborne branches. It was he who told our mother the story of the child who was offered to the wind."

"To live with the wind?" a child asked.

"In a way," said Mina.

"The Willow have made their peace with the Nir," said Esur.

"I knew the time would come. The Nir have many hands, many eyes. More wants more, my dears."

Esur spoke again, "The NesGras in the north were taken by the wind. Only a few men survived and they joined the Nir."

"The wind is hungry."

"As are the Nir."

"Our Willow brothers will join them in the spring. Others will connect with them, too. It will not be good for us to remain apart."

The family shifted into a tighter circle. Sura, small enough to be lifted, remembered fighting sleep. Her father's voice, resonant and rhythmic, told about a man called Eagle, a man who still lives. . . .

Now, living among the Nir, Sura strained to remember this story. She had drifted off to sleep during its telling, and her own dreams conflated with the voices of her mother, Esur, and Mina. She saw herself lashed to the tree to keep from flying away. There was a woman who disappeared after her baby was killed by the wind. The father of the child was named Tell, the eagle of the Nir. Could this be true? Could the old man made of sticks be the same who made a bargain with the wind?

Sura waited until she and Tehil were alone. "There is a story I heard when I was a child, but I can't remember how it ends."

"What kind of story?" asked Tehil, retching slightly from the putrid mixture she was using to tan a rabbit's fur.

"It is about your grandfather, I think."

Tehil looked up.

"It was in the time of the great wind, when all of the people of the Huul suffered from the bitter cold. A man called Eagle—this was when my mother's grandfather was still a child— offered his infant daughter to the wind. The infant's mother disappeared. . . ."

"Yes, that story," said Tehil. She stretched her rabbit fur on the frame that sat beside her. She slowly rose and threw the smelly tanning liquid some distance away from where they were talking. She walked back and studied her rabbit fur as if she expected to find an answer to a great mystery there.

Sura watched her. "Have I insulted you?" she asked Tehil.

"Why do you say that?"

"We are close, Tehil. I don't know why our families bear so much malice toward each other. This is not to say that you have treated me any less than a beloved sister, but even I can see that your people flourish and grow, and that the NesGras—all my father's clan—count no more than a pride of lions. I am glad to be a part of your great family, Tehil, and I want to know more about them, about you and Naki, and about your mother and grandfather, too."

Tehil looked around just to make certain, Sura suspected, that Alu was not listening from behind a tree and began the story of the first Alu, who was a gift to the wind.

"Tell was a young man in his prime. Kin to the eagle, everyone said. He had two children when his young wife died, and in the proper time, he took another woman who was small and beautiful, as the Willow women tend to be. She was quiet and deferred to Tell in everything, and in that, she was not like a Willow woman at all. You know the saying, when a Willow woman moves her mouth, we all move. It was during this time the wind set about destroying all the living creatures of the Huul—the hyena, the lion, the bear, the deer, the rabbits, the wolves, the foxes, the people. No animal was too large or small to escape its ravenous appetite. The people did their best to accommodate the wind. A tent with a fire in its center is as warm as a mother's womb, but the wind tore their sheltering tents from where they were fastened to the ground. They built fires in the open. They circled the fires with rocks; the rocks alone were warmed, and the people froze. The Willow woman became pregnant with her first child. It was not a happy event. There was no one left in the Nir camp who knew how to stop a pregnancy. Tell's Willow woman was young and weak, and even babies of the strong succumbed to the cold and harsh weather. And she was not strong. At first, no one noticed that her cycle did not come. She spoke to no one. Tell, perhaps feeling the life within when he approached her, knew first. Nevertheless, he tells us that he said to the wind, 'Spare us and you shall have the child of my wife.' Some scoffed. 'My child was taken and still the wind blows.' Others joined in. 'Does Tell think his child is a more satisfying meal than all the others the demon wind has devoured?'

"Tell shook with passion and entreated the wind to loosen its grip. He trembled and gyrated and hummed. The women of the camp began to dance around him, singing the song for the dead, dancing in circles until they fell to the ground and their eyes rolled back and they shook with the same palsy that afflicted Tell. Now what was strange was that Tell's wife did not shake or sing or fall. She seemed to be trying to become one with the shadows. She stood in the coldest recesses of the camp, braced against a tree to keep from getting tossed to the ground by the wind. In that bitter cold, she didn't move. If her cape slipped off her head, she took no notice. When the others, coming back from the nether world of the wind, would go and find her, her hair would be frozen, her eyes singed shut by the frost. Yet she endured, and in due time, her child was born. Alu. The first one.

"Spring did not come that year. Now, instead of the people of the tribe coming together to make decisions that affected them all, they waited for Tell to engage the wind, to make a bargain as our people have always done. I will give you my rhino cup, and you will give me your fine spear. A fair trade. Tell said, "I will give you Alu, and in return, you will not kill us as much.

"And Tell touched the wind. We all felt the wind, but only he could speak to it. And it spoke to him. To see him communicate with the wind, I dare not say as an equal, struck us all with wonder. I have seen him, Sura, and his possession is complete. And he is old now, but he was a strong, young man at this time. He does not breathe so that the wind would not be jealous of his breath. He does not eat or drink for many days before. He cuts his forehead and rubs the blood of an eagle into it so that he becomes the eagle. His voice is a caw, the screech of the predator swooping down on its prey. He dies while his spirit visits the spirit world and answers many of our questions about where our life goes. He knows when a tree dies, even as its leaves are green. He—"

Sura interrupted. "Tell me about the first Alu, please."

"The baby Alu was round and rosy and her mother was transformed. She spoke to her baby as if she was the only one who could understand her. Her breasts filled with nourishment, and the child was eager to suck. I tell you, Sura, it was hard to rip that infant away. Tell was insistent. Many of the women whose children had died as infants wailed in grief. The Willow woman threw herself on the ground, clung to Tell's feet, begged to die in her infant's place, struck herself with rocks, sucked the blood from her wounds, and spat it in Tell's face."

"Is this the way he tells it?"

"No. This is the woman's story. Tell speaks of her sadness, not of her disturbed spirit. Most of the people too sick and weary to endure another winter believed that Tell had interpreted the wind's intentions correctly. If the wind could keep its bargain, then so could they.

"Tell and his brothers approached the woman as she and the baby slept. As they were about to take the child, she woke up and tried with all her strength to hold on to the child. How could she? Tell had three living brothers and they overcame her. Her screams woke the whole camp. No one came to her aid. I asked why when I first heard the story as a child, and most say the wind itself held them in place. That and the fear in their empty bellies. Of course, except for Tell, there is no one alive who witnessed that terrible time.

"The men brought the infant to the top of the mountain and removed her fur wraps. As they did, the little thing woke up. She howled at the assault on her skin. You can still hear her cries when the wind blows."

"And the mother?" Sura asked.

"When Tell and his brothers returned to camp with the infant's clothing, she was gone. She took blankets and something else, too. Tell's long spear was gone. She followed their footsteps to the top of the mountain, but they say they never saw her ascend."

Sura shivered. "Did they ever look for her?"

Tehil looked away. "It is not told that they did."

"Did the wind keep its promise?"

"Not right away. The following year, when Tell had taken a second wife, the wind's rage abated. Winter still brings its harsh yield, as you well know. Its old intensity has dissipated, its hunger sated. I hope you are not more afraid of Tell now."

"Thank you, Tehil. I can't measure my fear right now. Something puzzles me. Men and women have made a bargain, too. Women bear the pain of bearing children, while men promise to protect them, even if they trade their own lives in the process. Did anyone question Tell's breach of that promise to Alu's mother? Did he offer the wind his own life as a sacrifice?"

"Sura, you are making my head hurt with your questions. Be satisfied that the wind did not kill you when you were alone on the mountain before my brother and cousins found you. Be grateful that Tell and our band have taken you in, even though your people chose long ago to remain apart from us because of that child. You wear the beads that Naki filled with his love for you. One day, should winter spare us, you and Naki may have a child who will be in Tell's line. If the wind had not been appeased, would any of us be alive? Respect what we believe, Sura; it will be easier for all of us."

Tehil walked briskly away. Sura told herself that she would reconcile with Tehil later. Questions flooded her mind. What happened to the Willow woman? Did she reach her child before the wind devoured her? Why did she take the long spear with her? Would the wind grow hungry again? While it was true that the Nir flourished since that time, the NesGras had shrunken to less than five bands within the territory of the Huul. Now the Nir had contacted her family and made sure they would come to the great gathering of the clans. She was the reason that they would come. Survival depended on the help of other people. Children were cherished and protected. Mothers could nurse two infants at a time so that a child who survived his mother would not starve. It was in no one's interest to weaken a nursing mother or to sacrifice a healthy child. Live to mourn your parents; that was the NesGras saying.

There were stories of clans who lost so many members that even their ability to hunt and make clothing, to build shelters and make fires, was lost. They lay on the ground, unable to remember why they were alive in the first place, until, to the last person, they died.

CHAPTER ELEVEN

GATHERING

Green shoots and small-capped mushrooms showed through the crystal webs of ice. Fresh water flowing north divided the Huul. Mountains stood like protecting parents on either side of the valley, nourishing it with running snowmelt and downward-drifting soil.

Willow families arrived first to build a large, open structure on the south shore of the lake. They raised a joyous shout of greeting and rushed to embrace the weary NesGras whose high mountain home kept ice the longest. Now that the cold was retreating, they were as hungry for each other's company as they were for the food withheld by winter. The four clans of the Huul would be together for the first time in many years: the Willow, the NesGras, the Wolf Moon, and the Nir, who outnumbered them all.

A Willow woman, her yellowed hair too sparse to plait, her skin loose on her bones like worn deerskin, sang an old song within a circle of clapping young people. When the old woman saw Mina, she raised her arms in greeting and the young people sprang to help her rise. Mina called her *aunt* because she was the sister of her grandfather, one of the few from that generation still alive. She stood up, steadying herself with her walking stick, and waved the young helping hands away. Mina hurried toward her. "Aunt, I'm happy to see you."

"Surprised that I'm still alive, Mina?" she asked, laughing.

"Yes," said Mina, who did not soften her words.

"Do you know why I am still alive?"

Mina shook her head. "No, but I am glad you are."

"I tell myself to keep moving," said her aunt as she tapped her arthritic knee. "No matter how much it hurts, I keep moving. That's my secret. Those young people would do anything for me." Her companions smiled in agreement. "Huh." She snorted. "They'd carry me if I let them. I say, no. Keep moving. There'll be plenty of time for rest when they lay a stone slab on my bones."

Even in her dotage, nothing grew in the natural world she could not name and assign a use or a warning. The old woman taught the young Willow to render sense in a world suspended in mystery.

"Is it possible you have grown since I last saw you," she asked Mina.

"I don't think so," said Mina.

"Then it must be that I have gotten smaller." She laughed at the joke on herself.

"Where is that man who always smiles?" She loved to tease Mina about Ququr's appearance.

Her aunt put her arms around Mina when she heard of Ququr's death.

"And the bear?" she asked.

"Consumed," said Mina.

"And the claws?"

"They weigh on Nin's shoulders."

"Then *nothing is lost*, is it?"

"As you taught me," said Mina.

She told her about Sura's disappearance and about the news from the travelers who passed through the Nir and the NesGras and all of the camps of the Huul. Sura lived because the Nir helped her.

"Then she will be here," the old woman said. Mina never doubted that she would. Sura's spirit reverberated between them now as strongly as if she was already standing there.

The Willow and the NesGras children, who had never seen each other before, fell into immediate and exuberant play, as if they had communicated plans for this time together when they were born. The girls took each other's hands to form circles for their games, while the boys broke through the circles as fast as their legs could churn up the ground. They reaped energy from each other; they leapt and tumbled as though the rocks and hard earth were cushioned with feathers. The fatigue they complained of on the long trek evaporated at the sight of other children spinning and screeching in the eternal language of child's play.

Before the people ate, they gathered close and bared their arms to the sun. They felt her blessing in the golden rays that turned the dun rocks to shades of yellow, pink, and orange. They prayed for protection against hunger, from the terrors that could strike from any direction, and they scattered the dust of the earth to the Spirit in all of its manifestations: to the east where the sun is born behind the tall mountains, and to the west where the land was lapped by the sea. They flung the earth to the demons of the wind in the north, and finally to the south where the warm breath of life sustained them at their birth. They looked at the faces around them and saw that many did not make the journey. Yet, new life bawled in their place, each child reinforcing their belief that nothing was lost that could not be renewed.

The first week of the monthlong gathering was beginning. The Willow from the north lived closest to the lake of the Huul. The NesGras were southeast, equally close, but had to move over mountains to reach it.

The Nir were far to the south, but the coastal plain along the blue-green sea afforded them level ground. The Wolf Moon were farthest on the rugged plateau, which was the southwest boundary of the Huul. Once descended from the high ground, they followed the banks of the saltwater lake deep in the low-lying valley. They would be the last group to arrive. The Wolf Moon clan, called howlers, squabblers, and rabbit catchers (and worse when they were not present) loved to tell stories where they were always swift, clever, and brave. And as much as they loved to tell them, their listeners loved to hear them. "Oho," they would exclaim, "did you hear how far the Wolf Moon man claimed he threw his spear? It went through the great sky Hunter's heart before striking the deer."

Gradually, as the story was repeated, the teller became a witness. "I did see it!" And the spear became a shooting star. "It hasn't landed yet!" Like their actual spear-throwing contests, the excitement of the farthest, the biggest, and the strongest lifted them high above the solid ground that held them fast.

In the distance, a crowd of strangers approached. The group came closer, and Xur could see that there were three women out front painted with ochre and charcoal in the manner of the Nir. One of the women broke from the group and ran toward him. Xur held his arms out wide. "Sura," he cried with joy as she rushed to embrace him.

The great group of Nir burst into the camp together to a great whoop of welcome. Mina, not forgetting her promise, removed the round pip shaped like a girl's face from her sack and placed it in the heart of a bonfire, watching as the smoke carried the prayer of gratitude to whatever power that allowed Sura to survive.

Within two days, all of the known people of the Huul were assembled on the southern shores of the lake. If any had misgivings about past quarrels, they were not voiced. It was best, the Willow thought, to treat the Nir like close family, to forget their long-ago differences. What happened between them was in the time of their grandfathers, the time during Tell's youth when they sheltered together during the great Ice Fall, before the wind broke their concordance. Yes, they forgot. It was best to forget. They had their own ways. And they have changed. The evidence of this is Sura's life and health. Now all the people—the Nir, the Willow, the distant Wolf Moon, and the contentious NesGras—could come together as they once did, before the wind drove them mad.

See how they join in the games. The grandsons of old Tell, Zuya and Naki, are entering into the circle of men. They will wrestle their bones against ours. They will laugh, whether they win or lose. See how different the Nir are from the old ones who embraced death. They would never again wipe the ground with their own blood to feed a hungry spirit. Only Tell was still alive from those days, except perhaps the old aunt who was a small child herself at the time. So no witness will come forward to object. All those stories. We are a people who tell stories; we paint pictures on the air with our words. Why, a picture of a bird cannot fly, can it?

And they buried their memories into hope for more feasts and greater gatherings and strengthening bonds between the Willow, the water seekers, the Wolf Moon, the sky readers, the NesGras, the hill dwellers, and the Nir, the people of the fertile shore.

The contest started. Xur faced Zuya, his Nir opponent, in the center of the clearing. Their eyes locked. They hunched their shoulders and swung their flexed arms in a shallow arc back and forth in front of them. The entire population of the camp gathered around them, children left off playing, and young men threw their spears down mid-competition to make their way to the front of the crowd. Xur and Zuya closed the space between them. The outer edge of Xur's right foot pressed against his opponent's. They leaned in with their shoulders against each other. They turned on the axis of their two legs that pressed together. Xur quickly brought his right foot behind Zuya's and flattened him on the ground. Xur lay across Zuya's chest and brought his left arm across his throat. The crowd howled with excitement. Esur and Manul looked at their sons and smiled. Nin, who pushed to the inner ring of the circle, suddenly screamed, "Xur, kill him!" They looked at Nin, their smiles washed from their faces, then went back to their cheering. Zuya pushed Xur's face away from him, bending Xur's neck into an arc. Xur flipped onto his back, and it was Zuya's arm that pressed into Xur's throat. Xur slapped his hand on the ground, a signal of surrender, and Zuya jumped up, arms upraised. Xur stood, coughed a little to show his throat really was hurt, and the crowd seemed overwhelmed with happiness. Two more wrestlers took their place and the scene was repeated: one triumphant winner, one humbled loser.

Bani found Nin far beyond the rim of the campsite. "Where have you been?" he asked. Nin's face lay buried in his arms. A sob escaped him. "Nin, why are you crying?"

"Why did Xur let him win?"

"Because we are grateful," said Bani.

"For what?"

"He is one of the people who helped Sura."

"Xur could have beaten him and he let him win."

"It's a game, Nin. Anyone with eyes could see that Xur is stronger."

"Now the Nir will think we are weak."

"No, they won't. They'll think we know how to be guests."

"Weak guests," said Nin, a look of profound hate coming over his square face as Bani helped him to his feet.

"Come on, Nin," said Bani, still holding Nin's hand. "We don't want to miss any more fun." Then he added, "Isn't it wonderful that Sura is with us?"

Sura grew tired listening to the formal talk between Mina and Alu and between Manul and Esur. Neither of the fathers had much to say beyond required greetings and salutations. Xur sat straight, as did Naki, who still managed to glance at Sura and at Xur's spear with equal avidity. It was agreed that Sura would remain with her own family for the coming year, preparing for the life of a woman and a Nir. Naki, the nimble carver of bone and wood, would hunt and gather not only for himself but also for Sura. Should they live through winter, she would join Naki and they would be a family in the camp of the Nir.

The Willow carried their decorations of shell and horn to the gathering, the Wolf Moon their supple leather and fur, the Nir their carvings of wood and bone, and the NesGras their shapely tools and sharp knives. They traded the objects with each other so that a Wolf Moon girl wore a collar of fox and a necklace of shell. A Willow man carried a NesGras blade on a leather belt crafted by his Willow cousin. Sura began to feel something that both disturbed and exhilarated her. Her replaced clothing, since coming to stay with the Nir, looked the same as the robe, shift, and cape that she wore when she started on her last walk with Xur. She made it herself, and while it was simpler than the clothing worn by Zamia and Tehil, the incentive to replace her ruined clothing was instigated more by the weather than by the mode of Nir craftsmanship. Now she looked around, and for the first time, she saw many other girls of her age. Her shift, a rectangle of leather wrapped simply around her body, was secured above her breasts and at her waist with a narrow band of leather. The cape she left behind to cover Xur was back on her shoulders. Her leggings, lost on her hard night alone, were Tehil's. She was aware of a new longing, not for her family or the companionship of friends, but a hunger to have what strangers were caressing: a refined cut of cloth, jewelry with no use except to excite the wearer, and more than one of something you didn't even need one of. Sura turned her round, wooden beads to feel their caress on her throat and felt that, somehow, it was wrong.

That night, while everyone slept soundly, warmed by the banked fires, though she tried to keep still, Sura's heart raced. Mina moved closer to her and spoke to her in a voice so low that Sura at first thought it was part of the dissonance in her head.

"A man feels life differently," said Mina. "He grows but he doesn't change. Before or after he has been with a woman, he is the same; it is not that way with a woman."

Sura's face burned, but she said nothing.

"When the time comes for a woman to bear a child, she changes. She is no longer *I* but *we*. She cannot disperse as the she-wolf sometimes does, content to join a pack or wander alone according to her whim. She needs a circle around her to help protect her child."

Mina continued.

"If she plucks a berry, her joy is not in the sweetness, it is in her child's delight in the berry. If the child is hurt, it is she who feels the pain. If her child dies—if all her children die— she is still a mother. What once grew beneath her heart lives there forever, not just a shadow or a memory, but the whole weight, forever. No man can know that."

Mina glanced at Sura's face.

"Don't be afraid, Sura. It is the only way."

The next night Mina told this story to the all the gathered people.

In the time before memory, when the people were giants and newly arrived from the campfires in the sky, a man and a woman lived in a land without trees. They were content because they had never seen a tree and therefore did not miss it. After a long time alone, they had a child whom they loved very much. They named him Gad and spent their days telling him the stories of people, spirits, animals, and plants that walked the dark land of the starry campfires. At night, they lay on the flat land and pointed to the tracks in the sky. "See, there is Grandmother Bear. She watches over her cubs just as we watch over you, dear Gad."

Gad grew into a kind boy who obeyed his parents and stooped with them to gather the arid vegetation upon which they fed. One day he spied a hill, a very unusual thing in his flat country, and as his parents rested, he went to explore what lay behind it. On the other side of the hill, the landscape undulated in a most unfamiliar way. Here, instead of the dry, flat earth that brought forth only the most meager of food, rabbits frolicked around tussocks of grass, fat birds hopped with worms wriggling in their beaks, and the blue of the sky was graced with white clouds, which Gad tried to reach by stretching his arms upward as far as he could.

He walked farther and farther from the familiar into this land. He stooped to drink from a stream that flowed and teemed with fish and turtles and water birds. In his reflection, the grass that waved just beneath the surface of the water seemed to grow from his own head. "If I could live here forever," he said. He pushed his toes into the loamy soil and raised up from his knees, reaching up so slowly that a bird lit on his head and placed a tuft of grass in his hair before flying off. After a time, he saw the clouds had disappeared, and the tracks of the sky were brightened by campfires that glowed and pulsated. On its black surface, he saw Grandmother Bear and he finally remembered. But when he tried to run back to his mother and father, he found that his feet had become roots and his limbs were hard, and in his brown and thrusting fingers, green leaves grew in startling abundance.

Now, his mother and father, seeing that it was dark and Gad was not there, became fretful. They ran in all directions at once. They ran until they were behind the hill. Because it was nighttime, and because their thoughts were only for the safety of their son, they saw nothing of the strange land-scape. Finally, they stopped, and when the sun rose in the morning, they saw it through an entanglement of green leaves and branches. They blinked their eyes at the wonder. "A tree," they said and touched its strong trunk and felt the hard limbs as if feeling the muscles of a young man.

"Mother, father," the tree said. They heard only the murmur of the wind caressing the high branches. Time passed, and they grew old in the shade of the tree. While they never forgot him, the wound that his disappearance had left dulled and closed. Gad's heart, which still beat with a boy's tenderness, wished that they could know it was he who sighed for their touch, but the spirits did not have the strength left to undo the transformation of Gad.

CHAPTER TWELVE

HYENA

The camp woke to great excitement.

"One night," a Wolf Moon man said, "I saw a spotted female hyena."

"How did you know it was a female?" asked an old man from the Willow clan.

"Because it was so big."

"How close were you to this female?" the old man asked.

"Be quiet, old man, and let him tell his story," someone shouted.

"We came upon a lion eating a fawn," said the Wolf Moon man.

The old man asked, "Who is we? You said only you saw the hyena."

The crowd grumbled, "Stop interrupting."

"We is the hyena and me," he said. "The hyena started to pace up and down, keeping its distance from the lion."

The young Wolf Moon man looked at the old Willow waiting for him to say something, but the old man just stood with his arms folded across his chest and his chin jutting out.

"Go on, tell us the story," the people around the fire called.

"The hyena whooped many times, over and over again. Another hyena came, then others, until a whole family stood shoulder to shoulder with a young one sheltered behind them. They moved forward, a phalanx of hyenas threatening the lion with their strange language."

The old Willow, unable to hold his tongue any longer, said, "I have known more than one who could speak the hyena's language."

This bit of information caused the group to pause as if searching their memories for hyena language speakers before the Wolf Moon man continued with his story.

"Usually," he said, "a lion pays no attention to a group of hyenas, but she became very alert to the hyenas' presence. Her ears flattened and she bared her teeth, growling deep in her throat. She dragged the fawn carcass under a tree. Suddenly, the hyenas made the most frightening sounds."

"How did they sound?" the young ones begged. And the young Wolf Moon man made the sounds the hyena makes at night, starting with a deep moan, rising in pitch, laughing in careening peals, until a child burst into tears thinking that the storyteller was himself a hyena.

"The hyenas' round ears rotated and aligned themselves toward the lion's warning growl. The hyenas' manes bristled on their muscle-humped shoulders, and their black tails curled over their backs as they edged toward her. The lion stood and faced them, growling fiercely now, ears flat, her yellow skull moving from side to side by the power of her voice. I could see all the teeth in her sinewy jaws as she fastened the dying deer with her claws."

He spread his hands. "Her stabbing teeth were longer than my fingers, sharper than our keenest blades. Her bite was swift. The deer was dead before it could cry out."

He lowered his voice. "The hyenas were quiet too now, bent on intimidating her, approaching her head on, ignoring the terrible warning in her yellow eyes. Suddenly, the lion lunged and let out a roar that shook the ground." This time, the young man did his best to imitate an attacking lion—*ROAR*, he bellowed, rolling his head like an enraged lion. "But the hyenas were fast. They moved in, and the lion, shaking her head more in annoyance now, turned around, crashed through the underbrush, and left the uneaten carcass for the hyenas to finish."

"That's impossible," the old man said.

"It's not only possible, I saw it with my own eyes," said the Wolf Moon man.

"Was the lion a runt?" he asked.

"The lion was afraid of the hyenas."

"How does a lion show fear?" a short Nir man wearing the mane of a lion at the neck of his cape asked. Everyone turned to look at him.

"He shows his tail." A young man laughed.

The lion-wearing Nir closed and then opened his eyes so slowly in the young man's direction that the crowd drew in its breath and didn't breathe out again until the languid blink was accomplished. He took a massive stone from somewhere beneath his cape. "The blood of this lion"—he fingered the yellow fur—"has never been washed from this weapon." They all stared at the massive, tear-shaped stone. "And I challenge any fool who doubts the courage of the beast who faced it."

Everyone looked cautious now. Who would challenge a wearer of lion skin, an imbiber of its blood, an admirable killer of the most admirable predator?

Another Willow man spoke. "Many times, I have seen lions take the kill from hyenas, even when there are many hyenas, a whole clan of hyenas, not just a small family."

"Many times," a few repeated.

"The hyena waits to finish what the lion disdains—fur, bones, even teeth," another added.

The old Willow man, impatient with the reasonable tone the conversation was taking, addressed the Wolf Moon man again. "Did the hyenas carry off the deer and hide it?"

The Wolf Moon man eyed the lion killer carefully while he answered, "No."

"And did you take your share?" the old man asked.

"What share was mine to take? It was not I who stalked the lion."

"True, true," they said. Others pointed out that hyenas do not stalk their prey. Everyone expressed an opinion. Hyenas, it was told, killed and ate unprotected cubs. No one had heard of hyenas taking on a full-grown lion. Did the lion fear the hyenas, and if not, why would she give up her prey to them? The lion man defended the lion's courage, but many attested to the courage of the smaller animal. The crowd thrilled at the controversy

this new story excited. Sides were drawn. How would this debate be settled? They argued through the night, creating and discarding rules for the
great hyena versus lion challenge. It would be a spectacle, a spiritual display, where the children would learn to understand the spirits that beat
in the hearts of the beasts that hunted the same prey as they. The lion, the
bear, the wolf were their respected kin, more like them, they believed, than
the hyena that never attacked or feared man. And while they had never
witnessed the ceremonies of their great fellow predators, they would create
one solely sprung from their collective imagination. Who could bring the
story to life? Who could move the way a lion moved? Who could fill the
night air with laughter so stirring that the hyena of the forest would come
to hear its story told? Who could prove to the gathered clans of the Huul
which of these animals possessed the greater courage, the better spirit to
which they, the human tribe, should aspire?

The lion could hunt alone or with only one or two companions. The
hyena hunted with its entire family. Should the hyena side have so many
participants? Did anyone know of a precedent that would limit the number? Everyone shouted at once. One man said that since a lion was the size
of three hyenas, there should be three hyenas and just one lion. The Wolf
Moon man who told the story agreed that it seemed fair to him. The lion
man gazed importantly at the space above the Wolf Moon man's head, then
nodded. The spirit of the lion was clearly chosen, but who among them
possessed the spirit of beast that laughed at the night?

By now, everyone at the gathering was joining the circle. The Wolf
Moon man stood facing the Nir lion man. The Old Willow man stepped as
gingerly as he could behind the Nir. Tell made his way to the center, leaning
on Alu's arm. "Who will defend the spirit of the lion?" More than half the
men raised their arms into the air. "Who will take the part of the hyena?"
More arms cleaved the air, but only one spoke: "I will," said Alu.

Now everyone shouted at once. People in the back of the crowd said,
"What? What? Did Alu speak?"

Tehil turned to Sura with a satisfied smile that said, "Who else?"

When Sura went to say good night to Tehil and Zamia, she could hear the spotted hyena's eerie cry from within Alu's shelter. She was glad that tonight she would sleep with the NesGras at the far end of the camp. Sura called from the outside, "May I enter," although she could see inside quite well. Alu was sitting in a most peculiar way. She was on her knees, but her weight was on her fingertips in imitation of the hyena's powerful and disproportionately large head, chest, and forelegs. Her smile spread her lips wide across her face but held no joy or humor. Her narrow nose was painted to resemble the black, upturned nose of the beast. Tehil and Zamia turned to Sura, and as they did, Alu howled, and the wild animal of the night seemed real and about to attack. The three girls leaped backward, shrieking, until the hyena, grunting as it metamorphasized back into Alu, stood up and stretched her arms.

"Get back in here," she told them, "I'm not finished. Stupid girls." Then she looked over her shoulder and announced, "I need a tail." She then marched past the girls who stood awestruck at the shelter door and made her way toward her father's hearth.

"Should I leave now?" Sura asked.

"Stay a little while, please." Tehil lowered her voice. "We are learning more than we wanted to know about the habits of the hyena. You would think that Alu was herself a hyena."

At that, the girls shuddered.

Alu reentered carrying what resembled a tail, switching it back and forth, first in front of her and then in back. "How can I attach it in back and still make it move," she said to no one. She fixed her eyes on Sura. "You're not so stupid," she said. "If the tail hangs down, they will think that I am cowardly," she said. "It must be animated. It must strike fear into that arrogant lion. He drank the lion's blood! Well, I have eaten the hyena's scrotum!

All hyenas, male or female, have a scrotum, a penis, and a vagina. They father their children and bear them, too. What other animal can say that?"

On the night of the great hyena debate, a row of fires burned in front of the pocked wall of the mountain that edged the western boundary of the camp. Except for the Nir lion man, Alu, and her family of hyenas, Tehil and Zamia, everyone gathered in a great semicircle, waiting for the performance to begin.

Tell appeared in front of the fires and spoke.

"In many ways, we are like the lions—our knives are our teeth. We use fire to help our eyes see in the dark."

"A lion has a fire in his eyes," someone said, and Tell nodded and continued.

"In many ways, we are like the hyenas. Our courage makes us grow so that we fool the lion into thinking we are bigger than ourselves. The Wolf Moon man witnessed a lion relinquish its prey, an act some believe is not in its nature. Can a hyena run faster than a lion? Can it run faster than a man?"

The crowd shouted their opinions all at once, excited by Tell's prodding.

"We will see the lion and the deer with the Willow man's eyes."

"I see the lion," a boy shouted, pointing to the lion man who stood in the shadows behind Tell.

"We will listen to the story so that our ears will hear what he heard."

Tell stepped back and disappeared into the darkness. The Wolf Moon man took his place and began his story, stepping aside to reveal the Nir lion man who held in front of him what appeared to be a small, freshly killed deer carcass. He brought it to his lips and took a big, dramatic bite. Something dark oozed from his lips and dripped from his chin.

"Ooo," said the crowd.

The hyenas approached: Alu and her cubs. The fires lit the performers from below yet partly obscured them. They cast gigantic shadows on the mountain wall, and the living flame danced and soared as if to break free of the hearths. Alu swung her arm, and an immense silhouette arced three times behind her; her raised foot echoed in staccato backlight behind them. The hyena, Alu, and her daughters were the whole pack, and the lion man was all lions— terrifying, beautiful, powerful. The small man wearing the lion cape leapt higher than the fire, his feet clearing the ground. But it was the lion that landed in a crouch, still clutching the bleeding deer in its claws. With a thunderous rumble in his voice, he roared, "Who dares take what is mine?"

The hyena's wild and terrible laugh answered him. A Nir woman screamed, "Alu, beware, the lion will kill you!"

The hyena laughed again, louder and deeper. The lion hugged the deer carcass close to him, threw his head back, and bellowed, "I *will* kill you!"

The hyena moved closer to the lion, prancing out of the shadows, looking over the fires toward the people who sucked in their breath, almost faint with anticipation. She looked beyond them, over their heads. *Look at me, look only at me*, she compelled them with a low, hyena moan. The ridge along her back stood on end, and her spots were ringed with fire. Her ears were round and stiff and did not fold against the onslaught of the lion's threat. The cubs hung back and watched, doing a little dance in place, leaning forward, their painted arms hanging stiffly in front of them, calling to each other, *hehehehehe—so this is what it means to be a hyena*. Alu jumped a graceful distance, a little closer to the lion's prize. The lion growled, lowering his head but not his gaze.

The hyena approached with her teeth bared, her ears down. Her coarse mane was like wind-flattened grass down her back, and although she was upright, her knees were bent, ready to spring forward. The lion, disdaining to notice her, took another massive bite from the deer still skewered on his claws. The hyena came close, then twisted her body toward the wall, her face turned toward the lion, her rump flicking its hair-tipped tail in provocation. The lion leaped again, straight up, and landed hard on his hind legs. Did the earth shudder? Did the mountain wall tremble like a cloth in the wind? The hyena twisted again, and her cubs danced in rapid little circles beside her. The Willow drummers pounded harder and faster, the Nir hummed louder and deeper, the Wolf Moon people keened and yipped, and the NesGras raised their hands above their heads and struck them together. And because they were in a valley and the mountains watched and listened, the stone echoed the music and the wind, riding the sea beyond the mountain wall, whispered its approbation. And the lion and hyena tribes listened to their stories in the far dark corners of the Huul.

Sura walked back toward Esur's campfire, filled with wonder. The air palpated with excitement. *Alu. Hyena.* She heard it over and over. *Yes. She was both.*

A group of Willow women stood separate from the crowd, laughing. One beckoned to her. Sura approached them. Willows were her mother's people. She must have seen them as a child, but in the dark, she recognized no one.

"Sura," one said, "so you are joining with the hyena's son."

Sura nodded.

"Naki has promised to wait for me," she said as mildly as possible. *Why do they laugh so?* she thought.

"Her son, yes," a second woman said, suppressing a titter.

"It is good to meet you . . . again," Sura said, and began to walk away.

"You are so grown and healthy, Sura," said the first woman, stepping closer to Sura, "so much like your mother before she joined the NesGras."

"You knew my mother?" Sura stopped and turned to them.

"And Mina, too, of course," said a third Willow woman.

But before Sura could ask more questions, the second Willow woman spoke again. "As did Alu. Perhaps they were too young to remember her."

Sura didn't contradict the women, but she knew that Mina would never have forgotten meeting Alu—not the Alu who was Naki's mother, not the Alu who was now refusing the entreaties of her audience to disclose the workings of her animated hyena tail. Stories before the days of Mina's great-great-grandfather were told and retold without a word of change, she believed. Clan lore could grow, as the story of the lion and the hyena did tonight, and nothing was forgotten.

"I know that the NesGras and the Willow had enmity for each other," said Sura.

"Oho," said the first woman, "*enmity*. Your promise with Naki is not the first time the fractious people of the Huul have tried to bring our families together"—she paused—"but you are obviously in a hurry to get back to your hearth. Please tell Mina that Lumi wishes her well, and I will look for her when daylight comes."

Sura's curiosity was an itch she couldn't resist scratching. If Mina knew Alu, and didn't tell her, there must be a reason. She wished she could see their faces. Were they teasing her?

"You know," said Lumi, reaching out to touch Sura's shoulder, "that Alu is a Nir living in the camp of her father. Even the willful NesGras know marrying within your own clan brings a curse upon the children of that union."

They were not laughing now. Sura could see the three women as shadows, pressing together, bending their heads very close to Sura and lowering their voices.

"Naki is a handsome fellow, as you've noticed. And Tehil, so tall and straight-limbed. It's hard to believe that the young Alu, despite her unwomanly height, was considered a good match for our clan. Don't you agree?"

Which contention were they expecting Sura to agree with? The women laughed again, sounding, Sura thought, more like hyenas than Alu. "So much like the black-haired woman," Sura heard them say, not waiting to hear which black-haired woman they were talking about.

"Ow," said Sura, stubbing her foot where Mina sat alone in the darkness beyond the light of the hearth.

"Mother," she said as she circled her arms around her, "I found you."

Mina laughed, and Sura was glad to hear that it was nothing like a hyena's.

In the hours before dawn, the raucous throb of the camp slowed to a settled heartbeat. Sura told Mina about meeting Lumi. "You were fortunate it was so dark," said Mina.

"There are so many people here," said Sura, "so many things to learn."

Mina threw a crooked branch on the fire, which flared and spit.

"Lumi said she knew you and Mother as a child, that you knew Alu as a girl," said Sura.

"Lumi carries so many tales, I wonder how she has the strength to stand up."

"Did you?" asked Sura.

"My Willow grandmothers knew Alu before we were born," said Mina. "She was younger than you are now when she went to live with the Willow called Two. Two already had two wives before Alu, but one died and the other disappeared."

"Like the first Alu's mother?" asked Sura.

"No," said Mina. "Neither of the women had children."

"Did they call him Two because of his wives?"

"No. They called him Two because he had two spirits that fought without stop"—Mina pursed her lips—"and neither one was . . . kind."

Sura tried to reconcile the formidable Alu, who imbibed the dual spirit of the hyena with a young Alu, sent to live with a man who had already used up two wives.

"Did Two die, Mina? Is that why Alu returned to her father's clan?"

"Yes, but not right away. When the usual period of waiting passed and Alu, who actually grew to be as tall as her husband in that time, did not conceive, Alu hunted and killed a hyena and," she said delicately, "ate all of its male and female parts."

"Yes," said Sura, "she told me that."

A look of surprise passed briefly over Mina's face.

"This caused a great uproar in the Willow band because she did this on her own. She never consulted the grandmothers and grandfathers or anyone else for advice. And what they considered most egregious was that she used Two's favorite spear because she said hers was too short and too dull to pierce the hide of the hyena. Two's spear killed the hyena, of course, but in the killing, the spear broke in half. It took, I was told, many people to keep Two from beating Alu to death. But while Alu was recovering, Two was found far south of Willow territory, the bite of the hyena visible on his throat, or so his family said. So you see, Alu had to once again become a Nir because no other clan would have her. Now I have told you all I know."

"Mina"—Sura crooked her neck so that she could see into Mina's face—"why do you think the Nir took Alu back? Why was she allowed to stay with Manul?"

Mina pushed the rocks that ringed the fire into a perfect circle with her foot. She smoothed the dirt between herself and the rocks, as if that was all that mattered in the world.

"Why is Alu so"—Sura searched for the right word—"different?"

"Sura, when the sun shows itself, the waters rise to greet it. Before Alu was born, the sun hid from Willow and Nir alike. My grandfather was a Willow. Like the NesGras, he did not agree that Tell was more favored than other men. The wind, he reasoned, took what it wanted and spit the rest out."

Before Sura could ask any more questions, Mina told her another story, about a mother bear who loved her lost child so much, she turned into stone waiting for its return.

CHAPTER THIRTEEN

TELL'S MOON

Bani sat as close to Tell as good manners allowed. There were so many people trying to see the incised bone that Tell held. Were all of the young people of the Huul gathered in this one place? Bani looked around. He could see Xur and Nin. Xur waved to him from the middle of the crowd. Sura sat with her Nir friends, whose names he couldn't remember. All three girls wore their hair done up in the same way: shiny with oil and streaked with yellow. How much alike they looked. He liked the old Sura better. The NesGras Sura.

Bani was one of the youngest there. He was afraid that he might be told to leave and go play with the children, but so far, no one said anything to him. He could see the clan markings of the Wolf Moon, the Willow, and, of course, the Nir, Tell's people. There were no other NesGras except for his own family. What did the wizened old man know that so many wanted to learn? Tell waited, as still as a dead tree, for everyone to give him his full attention. Bani hoped his face didn't betray his excitement and fear. Was he the only one who knew so little about the bone? Their collective breath buzzed like a swarm of insects—the sound the air made before a storm. No one shouted as they would do during an ordinary performance or a wrestling contest. A few whispered but kept their eyes on Tell. People were still coming, scooting down to sit with their legs crossed as soon as they reached the edge of the gathering. They cradled smooth pieces of antler and wood, some with peculiar markings on the flat surfaces. Bani regarded his empty hands; too late now to find his own blank.

Tell raised his right hand and there was silence.

"What do I hold?"

The slim, dark boy sitting next to Bani stood up. He spoke very softly, "It is a calendar."

"It is a calendar," Tell repeated so that even the latecomers in the back could hear. "And what is a calendar?"

The boy looked as if speaking once had drained him of all of his energy and he sat down again.

"It shows us . . . ," a young woman started, but lost her nerve before she completed her answer.

". . . when to hunt," someone with a clear voice finished for her.

"And how does this calendar show us when to hunt?" Tell asked.

Bani could feel his heart pounding in his chest. How did a piece of wood or bone with marks in a random pattern show you *when* it is time to hunt?

Tell stepped closer to Bani and handed him the bone.

"What do you see here?"

Bani's ears burned. Words came out of his mouth, but he scarcely was aware that he spoke. "Many circles," he said.

"And what do the circles mean?"

Someone started to shout the answer, but Tell ignored whoever it was. Did he say moons? "Go on," said Tell.

"Moons?"

"Yes!" Tell said. "Moons."

Suddenly, the incisions on the bone were not circles or parts of circles. The night sky, no, the sky over many nights, appeared in his mind's eye—the full moon, the half moon, the crescent moon. The entire cycle moved in a curving swoon, then repeated itself. The lunar calendar was laid out in the pattern of a snake that turned and devoured its own tail only to emerge again. Bani could see it; the circles were the one moon that he studied every clear night. This bone showed the phases of the moon. It was a guide to the seasons. These peculiar marks were the summers to come, and the summer before, too. The moon was alive and traveled a certain path, and man could capture its path on a solid, lifeless object. It spoke to him in a way the actual moon in the night sky could not.

Before this meeting, the NesGras thought of the Nir as the malevolent characters in a tale to frighten children. They avoided each other for a long time. Bani would not be there now if Sura hadn't gone off in the wrong direction. Yet, from their separate places in the Huul, both the NesGras and the Nir watched the same moon and hunted on the same luminous nights. This incised bone could help them track the migrations of the horse and the ibex and could help them stay out of the way of the waking bear and the rampaging aurochs. Not that his father was less of a hunter or tracker than any man there, but here was something powerful beyond the massing of far-flung peoples, something more than the trading of tools and adornments. Bani could not yet articulate what it was about being one among many that engorged his spirit. He was filled with longing and anticipation.

Was the bone handed to him first because he sat nearer to Tell, or was he singled out? He tried to remind himself that not only did he repeat what someone else said, but he didn't carry any of the tools many of the older boys and girls carried. Yet here he was, holding a perfect depiction of the moon traveling over many nights. It felt alive and hot in his hand. A luminous spur to his senses.

Tell took the bone from Bani and moved among the others, asking questions and pointing out mistakes made by the novice inscribers. If the calendar had been carved into his own palm, Bani could not have seen it more clearly. Despite the real sun moving overhead, the phases of the moon swirled in rapid succession in his imagination. His hands ached to limn the advance of time on the durable substance of rock or bone or wood.

Many of the young people were getting up and going on to other areas of the camp. Only a few remained. Tell beckoned to them and a tighter, smaller circle was formed. An older Wolf Moon boy sat next to Bani. A tall Nir girl took her place next to the boy. Someone handed Bani a smooth blank and a burin—a sharpened antler to incise the image of the moon. He thought about what Mina said, "More wants more." But he forgot it was a warning and not an invitation.

"Now," said Tell, "who can tell me what this is?"

CHAPTER FOURTEEN

BLUE

The north wind spun feathers of ice in the winter sky. The cold froze hands and feet, turning exposed fingers and toes to obsidian, black and insensate. Keep the fires going was the essential rule for survival. Mothers carried babies heart to heart, under their wraps, wary of any changes in the temperature of the small bodies. Fevers rose fast, then broke in rushes of sweat that could turn to ice. A roseate, sucking infant in the evening could shrink and grow cold by morning, depleted and desiccated. Stilled, it was swaddled in a tiny burial shroud and laid under a mound of stones, the ground too hard to penetrate. The wind blew from a place grudging any comfort. The howl of the wind challenged the bay of the wolf, the bellow of the elk, and the shriek of the hawk. The wind always ate first and got its fill.

Outside the hollow, NesGras cave, a voice emerged, carried low on eddies of white air. The voice was guttural and plaintive, human but strange, an unknown peril rousing them to gather near the arch of the entrance. They stood, the youngest in back, the strongest in front, listening to the footsteps and the rasp of something heavy being dragged across the rime. It came closer. The men and women gripped their weapons and pressed together, focused toward the sounds. Whoever or whatever it was coming toward them was breathing hard. A hand emerged from the brush and took hold of a narrow trunk of a birch. A man of great height pulled himself to the edge of their camp. They stared, more startled than afraid. On his back, like a great cape, he bore another man who, in every way, was his twin. The man called again in his strange voice and slid the unconscious twin on the ground in front of him. As he did, the mantle he wore fell behind him, revealing his shoulders marked in vivid patterns of blue. His hair was as ragged as the manes of wild horses, without color, like people who lived beyond their own generation. His eyes, rimmed in red, were the gray of crystals that formed on the winter sea. His weapons and tools hung from a worn belt tied to his waistcloth. Except for these, he wore little protection from the cold.

Esur took a step toward the men. Xur and Rosh moved with him. Esur addressed the standing man, who growled and sputtered, gesturing to the twin on the ground. Mina, without a word, knelt beside the man on the ground.

The group moved closer. Rosh took his outer blanket from his shoulders and covered the unconscious stranger. The man raised the head of his twin, and Mina tried to give him water. Esur spoke to him in the formal language of greeting visitors, but the sounds the stranger made bore no resemblance to a language he knew. The twins, large even in their starved state, unmarked by the clan scars of any of the people of the Huul, were nonetheless taken inside the shelter. The NesGras could do nothing more than share their food and water and give them blankets to ease their rest.

The sick twin lived only a week, despite his brother's care and Mina's medicine. The man cried inconsolably, his ribs distending and contracting in grief. In the short time before his brother died, he tried to communicate, perhaps to tell where he was from or where he was going. Now he only sobbed, without kin to share his grief.

Esur and Rosh helped carry the dead twin into the recesses of a high cave and left his body with his brother to perform whatever ablutions the strangers required. The solitary man came back hours later. The next day, they moved on and he went with them. He walked at the rear of their small column, standing bear-tall, indelibly marked with the mystery of his origins. Despite the hardships evidenced by his ravaged appearance, he seemed to thrive. In the middle of the night he would sometimes weep, but he never spoke a word that they could recognize, hearing only what seemed to them like the crunch of nuts in a too-full mouth. They sensed the loneliness that ate him from inside, even as his strength increased and his stride quickened.

He made spears that found their marks unerringly. Both his skills and instincts matched theirs, and Esur especially seemed unaware of the absence of a mutual spoken language. While Esur's family shivered in the cold and held their wraps tightly around them, the stranger hunched on the ground and deftly spun a stone into a sharply pointed awl. He turned his pale face to his companions and smiled, and they, in turn, nodded and smiled back. He found the hollow bone from the thigh of a bear. He worked a small hole in the bone, then held it to his mouth and blew through one end. It whistled like the wind blowing through a thawing marsh. Everyone turned their attention to him. He spread his fingers apart and wrapped them around the bone. He kept his second finger on a spot near the first hole, studied the spot where the finger touched, and took up his awl to pierce the bone again. Blue, as they called him now, deftly turned another small hole and then another, and this time when he expelled his breath, he moved his fingers over the holes and the tones harmonized.

"What magic," Bani exclaimed, and Blue handed the bone to him.

"Music," he said.

Bani and Nin repeated, "Music."

First Nin then Bani puffed their cheeks and stretched and wiggled their fingers over the holes, and the sounds they made were terrible to hear. Soon all the children of the camp begged to have their turn, pulling in their breath with great heaves of their small chests, puffing up their cheeks, their eyes squeezed shut with the great effort of making a sweet noise. The adults, Sura among them now, could barely wait for darkness when Blue would wipe away the child spittle and mud left by small hands. Settling around the fire, he would play his flute as the people spoke softly until dozing off, their dreams carried aloft by the soft wings of music.

On an evening with the smell of spring blowing through the trees, Blue and Mina sat together before the fire. Blue sat hunched over, his chin resting on his drawn-up knees. Mina sat close to him and watched the side of his face. Tears trembled in his white lashes. He did not blink. Mina put her hand on his arm, and he turned to face her. He stood, and as she rose to stand with him, he put his hand on her shoulder to signal that he wished her to remain there. She looked up. No rain or snow, no windswept clouds curtained the stars that crowded the night sky.

Blue came back with a cluster of small branches taken from the kindling gathered that morning. He held them in his fist, pressing them to his chest. He kneeled and bent his body forward. He put the branches down in front of him. He took two sticks from the pile and lay them together, side by side. Then he put four more sticks beneath them. Finally, he placed three pairs, smaller than the rest, forming a bottom row. He regarded his arrangement, then moved the sticks closer so that they touched each other.

"Tell me," Mina said. Blue motioned with his hand to the rough circle where the rest of the family was in sleepy disarray around the fire. He pointed to Mina before clenching his fist to make the sign that meant both *family* and *together*.

Mina nodded. *Yes.*

She repeated Blue's gesture, taking in everyone in the camp, clenched her own fist, and brought it to her heart. "My family," she said.

When she reached for the branches, Blue gently closed his hand over hers to keep her from touching them. He picked up the smallest twigs in the bottom row. He pressed them to his cheek and held them to his lips, holding them as tenderly as a parent holds a child. Mina, the painter of cave walls, knew that these sticks were the means for Blue to tell his story. She just had to listen with her eyes to find out what it was.

Blue lay the little sticks in the shallow depression he scooped out in the ground and spread loose dirt over them. He repeated this ritual until only two identical twigs remained in front of them. He picked one up and pointed to the direction from where they had recently traveled, the direction of his brother's grave. He placed this twig beside the others and put some small stones over it, just as his dead brother lay pressed with stones not far from them.

The last he held and pointed to himself. Mina understood. Just as she lived surrounded by kin, so had Blue lived among his people. Now they all lay buried and he alone remained. She took the last twig that was Blue from his hand and placed it on her open palm. She reached beside her for a stray piece of kindling and pointed it at herself. "I," she said, "Mina." She placed the two, side by side, and closed her fist around them. *Together,* she whispered to Blue. She looked into his face. His eyes, dark now in the darkening night, held her eyes, blacker still. The darkness compelled them closer, until just outside the circle of light, they came together. Mina took the stranger Blue into herself and he covered her. His skin was warm, and their breath mingled in the cool, night air.

Nin stirred from his sleep and saw the rising and falling shadow across the embers of the fire. In the morning, he felt agitated and tried to remember the dream that so disturbed him. When the other children that day clamored to play the flute, he walked away, alone and sullen, unhappy in a way he never was before.

CHAPTER FIFTEEN

LION

A rumble deeper than the roll of thunder shook the forest. No weak and wounded human had tracked their camp this time. The people again formed a protective ring around the smallest members of their group, but now the stranger stood with them. The rumble resounded and became a low roar, and a lioness crept into their vision and crouched before them. Black streaked her yellow coat, the color of the shade-dappled boulders where she lived; the better to fool her prey, for she was prey to no one. Her muzzle furrowed, and she emitted a low growl. Her flesh-ripping canine teeth were as long as a man's finger. Her long tail, a tuft of black hair at the tip, swept across the ground behind her like a snake ready to strike. She fixed them with her yellow eyes, the black pupils vertical slits against the twilight. The people stood as still as stones, rooted by fear. They believed a cat could see you only if you moved. How long can you hold your breath? Or stifle a child's cry?

Before they could retreat, a second lioness cleaved the air and crashed into their vulnerable center. In confusion, their balance lost, they scrambled to grip their weapons and regain their puny stance. The first beast bounded into the unshielded middle, and in the raised dust and flailing limbs, tore an infant from the startled mother's arms and was gone without a sound.

The people fought valiantly with what they had, but spears and digging sticks, even when they managed to pierce the yellow hides, broke into pieces. The lion who had taken the infant was back. The two beasts rushed and feinted the cornered people, shaking off the shallow wounds, unfazed. Sura saw that Zu's girl, Hyssop, was now unprotected, and she ran toward her to snatch her into the cave behind them. As the lion primed to leap, the stranger thrust himself between the girl and attacking beast. Each lion weighed as much as two men, and the impact slammed him hard to the ground. The lion stood over him and opened her mouth wide. Blue rammed his arm down the lion's throat and ripped through from inside, the blade still gripped in his swallowed hand. Sura sat stunned for a moment, then pulled up, hugged Hyssop to her chest, and ran into the cave. She looked out and saw Xur, Esur, and Rosh struggling with the second beast. She screamed for Mina, who was pushing the rest of the children deeper into the cave. Blue struggled, his body crimson with blood. Unable to bite, choking and angry at the death and pain caught in her throat, the lion tried to maul the stranger and dislodge the hand that still held the knife. Xur, his father, and Rosh drove off the first lion and turned to help Blue. Xur's spear tore through the side of the lion, who spun blindly and collapsed on her side. Blue's arm, bitten off just below his elbow, spewed blood. He stared at the three men in shock. They looked back. No, not dead yet.

All were bruised and bloody. Ribs were painfully cracked, and Rosh's collarbone protruded at an oblique angle from his shoulder. Zu sat staring, not noticing her cradling arm hanging limp and broken from the lion's lunge when it took her infant. No one cried. Breathing was hard enough. Later, they would count themselves lucky that so many survived. Now they stood on earth, muddied and red. The throbbing physical pain and profound exhaustion drove all fear and sorrow to a deep and hidden place where it could transform into something they could confront at a later time. They braced their bodies as best they could. Mina couldn't tell how much blood Blue lost. *Not as much as the lion,* she thought. She tied off his wound, and whether he was in shock or understood the futility of crying out or even moaning, he was silent, his eyes on her face as she cauterized the injury and packed snow on the enormous lump on the back of his head. She pressed her ear to his chest and was surprised by its strong thumping. "Blue," she said, "you will live."

They ate what they could and took the incisors and claws so the great beast could not avenge herself after death. Then they left the carcass to the hyenas, the great enemies of the lion, and moved on, trying to keep the wind at their backs.

CHAPTER SIXTEEN

PROMISE KEPT

In the spring, the NesGras and all the clans of the Huul met as they had done the year before. Objects were exchanged, marriages arranged, new babies were admired. Mina's aunt had stopped moving at last. Her young people pointed to the night sky and singled out her campfire from the countless network of lights.

Sura looked up at a small mouth in the new, green face of the mountain. It seemed to be singing. It was one of many caves, some no more than niches in the rough breccia of rocks and ancient reefs, connected within the dark interior of the mountain like arteries to a beating heart. Sura's cave was entered by a mantle jutting above the rough path. She would go there with Naki before leaving for the Nir camp. According to Mina's directions, Sura gathered the buds of wildflowers to sweeten the slate floor that would be her bridal bed. She climbed into the cave and looked around at the gray walls. She used a branch to sweep the webs and nests from the uneven surfaces. The floor was smooth, sliced from the rock in the time outside memory when the ocean crashed above the mountain crests. In the floor, ancient fish left obdurate impressions of their small lives, like footprints in the sand.

When the last mouse was swept out and the sweetest petals replaced their droppings, Sura looked around the hollow chamber. Tomorrow, after the meal and the trading of gifts that manifested their union were done, after she and Naki spent the night in the womb of the rock, after marking her with the sign of that union, and after one final farewell with her kin, she would live as a Nir.

A wolf howled, and from a place far away, a wolf responded. Sura raised her voice. The three voices came together, three separate strands that curled around each other like smoke, echoing softly and disappearing before starting again. All who heard listened hard, feeling the sound in their own breasts. While some were afraid and took the call as a threat, others felt strength and a stirring of their blood. To them, the song of the wolf was the most beautiful music they had ever heard, an accompaniment to their mutual journey over the uneven landscape.

"It's morning," said Mina.

Sura sat up and reached for Bani, then remembered that he now slept with Esur and Xur, the men in the camp who lived without women. She felt nearby for a stick and stirred the embers. Nin, who was exactly Bani's age, still slept near his mother. *A tree stump*, thought Sura, and she meant it as praise for Nin's strength and stolid likeness to his father. One by one she committed the rising figures to her memory. This would be the last time that she would lie among the small group that was her female kin: Mina, who had become her mother after her own mother died, and Zu, the sweet Willow companion to Rosh.

She reached for the rootstock that was buried in the embers, tossing it from hand to hand. Mina deftly caught it and placed it back in the fire.

"Not today," she said. Mina carried the articles that would clothe Sura for the ceremony. Tehil and Zamia woke up and rushed from their campsite. "Today we are sisters," they said, but at the moment, she felt like a stranger even to herself.

Sura's clothing was laid out on the floor of the cave. For her throat, the feathers of an owl to call the moon into the sky. A shawl of deerskin draped her hair and shoulders, winding softly around her body to shield against a spirit jealous of her strength and youth. A skirt of weeping willow flowed over her hips, brushing the earth, which was her Mother, her provider, and her final bed. Her hair smelled like rosemary, a scent so rich and deep that it had weight and color. She carried briars in a pouch, sharp reminders that no path was without thorns, and an unworked stone as an admonition: *nothing is lost.*

She would take with her a new digging stick and an awl that Esur shaped from horn. For Manul and Naki, wrapped in a square of chamois, Xur carved points of jasper as green and finely etched as the leaves of spring. Each member of her family prepared a gift. Bani's was a bone pipe, improvised from a bird's delicate femur, a miniature replica of Blue's music.

"How many birds did we eat for that," teased Xur, who watched Bani's countless attempts before a single note could be formed. The sound was sharper and less varied than the aurochs bone flute, but it resonated pleasantly enough when put to the lips.

Stories were told in turn by Esur and Manul, by Alu and Mina, while the children tried to snatch pieces of the honey agaric before the elders finished their say. "Not yet," the grown-ups hissed, but they, too, eyed the hare on the spit, the nuts crushed between two rocks and mixed with treacle. Speckled, brown eggs, eggs with shells of palest green, and tiny eggs the blue of a winter sky all waited in carefully assembled stacks. Dried, salted fish from the Nir of the southern shore of the Huul and rough grains from the valley between the mountains were simmered in leather sacks to make them soft enough for everyone, from the very young to the very old, to eat.

Naki and Sura sat side by side but did not look at each other. Mina and Alu sat apart but snatched glances at each other whenever the other looked away. Xur leaned forward to touch Naki's shoulder from time to time, and Bani seemed on the verge of tears. Rosh's wife wept openly, while Hyssop scanned the gathered faces for friends from last year. The two families exchanged news, but they loved hearing the familiar stories best. Details were added or lost, like a clump of earth that picks up leaves and twigs as it rolls down a hill and sometimes loses pieces of itself as it tumbles down.

Night fell. Sleep overcame all but the determined young men who still shouted bawdy encouragement to Sura and Naki who made their way up the sloping hill side by side. The cave was redolent with lavender. For a while they stayed that way, touching, not moving, listening to the diminishing cries from below. Naki turned toward Sura and put an arm across her uneasy body. She tried to will herself to look at her new husband, wanting to turn toward him. She could almost see herself from above, like a corpse decorated for the grave, her desire for Naki compressed into a hailstone lodged below her belly. Naki gently moved until he was above her, his elbows supporting his weight, his hands cradling her face, whispering, touching his lips to her cheek. Her legs lost touch with her head and fixed themselves as if they were two logs lashed together, inanimate and insensate. Her unyielding arms stayed rigid alongside her body, despite the compelling warmth of Naki's touch. She slipped into sleep and woke to find Naki, who could no longer prop himself up, had collapsed atop her, his arms akimbo on either side of her, his head heavy against her shoulder. She stirred and Naki roused at once, bringing his arms under her head. Warmth surrounded and filled her. Her arms and legs encircled him; her face pressed itself to his. Their separate bodies vanished and became one, joining past and future, spirit and flesh, memory and oblivion. As the last ember cooled, the stone inside her melted, gone forever. The voices of the people faded, and the stillness of the night deepened. Invisible in the dark beyond, the great sea murmured approbation. Wave after wave unfolded on the sand as the sea covered the shore, then withdrew its foamy embrace.

CHAPTER SEVENTEEN

WOLF

From the ledge, Bani could see the great sea. Bands of blue and green rippled around boulders that hunkered along the coast. A cave chiseled by ancient waters yawned behind him. Above the jagged pinnacle of the coral mountain, clouds formed and reformed, competing to embellish the beauty of the fickle sky. He cupped his hands over his mouth and nose so that his breath would not mingle with the air and alert the creatures hiding below. Two ravens circled and cawed a dialogue about this intruder who lay as still as stone. Bani slowed his breathing to match the rhythm of the thorn bush stirring imperceptibly in the breeze.

Twilight formed a dark halo around the clouds, effulgent with orange and shimmering gray. Bani was unsure if he slept in the intervening hours between day and dusk, or if time melted along with the bright blue of the sky. The ravens swooped to the valley below and focused their raucous attentions on a family of wolves walking in a single line. A young wolf leapt at a raven that fluttered just out of reach of its snapping jaws. The arrogant bird flew up and shrieked with spiteful glee. Bani watched until they were out of view, then ran back to camp. He kept the sighting to himself and lay down, too excited to sleep. He strained his ears for the wolves' lamentation, but the howl of the wind ruled the night. He waited for dawn to return to the trail left by the wolves.

Bani had seen ten wolves, but when he returned to the trail, he found evidence of only two or three. He walked in the impressions left behind by the traveling pack. Snow drifted into great mounds crusted over with ice. He sank deeply into the underlying powder, plucking his leg from one deep hole only to stumble ungracefully into another. He studied the round, wide marks left by the paws of the wolf as they stepped into the hollows in the snow created by the lead wolf. Unlike Bani, their weight was distributed over four limbs, and their great, cushioned paws allowed them both grace and traction in the hilly terrain. Bani followed the trail, aching to know more about the wolf. The next day, Bani prepared to travel farther from his home camp.

Xur awoke and saw that Bani's sleeping robe and tools were gone. He left an unfinished digging stick pointing in the direction that he would take. This was their sign that the other would not return before nightfall. Xur regarded the direction, northeast, and pulled his robe tighter around his shoulders. He threw a piece of wood into the fire and remembered when he was Bani's age, setting out on his own for the first time.

The memory of the hunger that squeezed the muscles in his legs and shoulders and clenched around his temples was still vivid. Xur had been afraid and wanted only to let go of his spear and curl against the earth as he had once pressed against his mother's body as a small child. He crept into a shallow cave high on a hill. The floor of the cave had an opening the circumference of his head. Below the hole, light penetrated, and he could make out a hibernating bear. Xur was about to leave and look for a more comfortable place to wait out the night when he saw the bear gyrate in a most peculiar way. The bear, still sleeping, was undulating her body as if trying to throw off her skin. He was amazed. He heard the cry of a newborn, a squeal, a snuffle, a louder squeal. He poked his head into the hole in the cave floor and looked. Where was the baby? The cries grew louder, but still he could see nothing though he stretched his neck as far as it would go. It was getting darker, and the bear continued in its solitary struggle. In the last light, Xur could see a tiny hand attached to a small and very hairy arm swimming weakly in the fusty air. He squinted and saw a brown head wobbling free from its sleeping mother's womb, crying still, a baby, surely, a newborn cub, climbing to reach its mother's breast to suck from her as she lie motionless, saving strength for spring when she would clamor back to life.

Xur stayed and fell asleep at last. That night, if he dreamed, he did not remember. But many nights, he saw not a bear but a human baby emerge from the mother bear. And when he heard the cries, he awoke very sad and confused. He could have snatched that baby bear without waking its mother. He could have made a small and gratifying meal from its tender remains and used the sharp claws to clear his teeth of meat. When he would tell this story in both its dream and reality forms, his listeners would attempt to solve the mystery of the transformed baby, or the uneaten bear, responding in ways that Xur found unsatisfying, although he politely thanked them for their thoughts.

On the sixth morning, Xur's dread and hunger lifted. A track left by a red deer, invisible the day before, appeared bold now, simple for him to read. He thanked the spirits as they returned into the earth, pulling the darkness of the night behind them. Xur went back to his family that day with the deer lashed to his back. He learned to withstand the craving for food, but until this moment, he had forgotten the fear that went before. Now it was Bani's turn to learn the lessons of solitude. Xur suffered the pangs of hunger and loneliness for his brother, but Xur's sympathy could never be voiced. For Bani to survive, he had to learn to rely on himself when alone, and yet act as if he were a finger on the hand of his group when they were together. Once past babyhood, it was frowned on to cry from pain or fear. The lesson was evident: those who indulged themselves with such expressions were the first to succumb to the harsh life among the stones. There were solitary figures, men who chose to remain apart, who would douse their fires and move away at the approach of a familial band. There were stories about them, some admiring, some filled with fear. Capable of remaining alive in a wilderness of beasts and poisons, what sustained their hearts and minds without the touch of other humans?

Bani followed the trail of the wolf pack for two days, occasionally coming upon the remains of a kill. He consumed what little was left after they ate their fill. Like man, the wolf would scavenge the carcasses left by other predators. They hunted the diseased, the old, and the weak when they could, and like man, they pursued the strong and the agile for no other reason than to try their own strength.

Bani supplemented the chance meat with nuts and seeds gathered before the deep cold swept in, and with an occasional small animal unlucky enough to cross his path. He was single-minded in his pursuit of the wolves. He would follow them until he found the reason they lived in the form of their common father, the hunter of the night sky.

On the third day, Bani awoke with the feeling he was not alone. He turned his head to see a wolf sitting not very far away, its head tilted like an inquisitive child, looking at Bani with golden eyes boldly rimmed in black, the wind ruffling its dark-gray fur. Bani slowly sat up and backed up against the mountain wall. The wolf, without raising its hind legs, sidled forward on its haunches. Bani realized that while he followed the wolves, they had been leading him in a circle. If he followed the arc of their trail, he would be back to his home camp.

Like a boy, where caution is exceeded by curiosity, the young wolf approached him. Bani pressed his back to the mountain and stood up slowly, his hand covering the haft of his stone knife. Bani's eyes moved from the eyes of the wolf to its narrow chest, its splayed front legs, its great paws. The wolf, close now, leapt up, rested its front paws on Bani's shoulders, and began to lick him around his mouth. Startled, Bani shouted, "I have no mother's food for you, Wolf!" He wiped his mouth, pushed the wolf from his face, and laughed.

All day, they played as the young of all kinds do, trying out their skills and the limits of their agility. They shared food for which the wolf waited as Bani dispensed it. The wolf made low, snapping sounds, clearing its throat when Bani came too close to the bone that it held in its teeth, a warning not to overstep the boundaries of their companionship.

Bani ran only half as fast as the wolf, who would double back again and again. Bani took this as a game of hide-and-seek. The wolf, the superior hunter, would be behind Bani or next to him, scanning the landscape in the same direction that Bani looked for him, surprising him every time.

They used up the day in joyful abandonment, and when the day ended, Bani forgot his questions and fell fast asleep, silent and secure. The next morning, Bani awoke hungry and alone. Except for the disturbed ground, he would not have believed that the day before had happened. He went off to secure his breakfast and was finishing the last of it when he saw his companion appear.

"Today I have some mother's food for you," said Bani, as he offered the heart of a grouse. The wolf swept it out of his hand with its rough tongue and swallowed it, then sat back and looked at Bani expectantly. The questions came to him and then receded. They were questions for the spirit wolf to be addressed at another time. In the cold, morning light, the warm breath of the wolf was an invitation to run again. Bani buried his fire, secured his tools and clothing, and continued home, this time not alone.

Bani hastened behind the wolf to lower ground. They reached a wide expanse of red dirt and broken rocks showing through a lattice of partially thawed ice. The wolf stopped, pressed its snout against the ground, then bolted east. Bani ran fast, but the wolf was off in the distance, chasing behind what appeared to be a small deer. Bani accelerated, straining to see the wolf and deer as they diminished on the horizon. He pumped his legs and arms, breathed through his open mouth, and kept his balance, though his feet landed crookedly on the jagged rocks. His legs and arms pumped in the air for a moment even as he realized that the ground beneath him was nothing but dry branches—a blind trap for heedless prey. Bani grasped at the branches as he fell, the bottom a terrible surprise that blasted the breath and sight out of him. He lay stunned in the shadowy depths. He moved tentatively. He was bruised, but not broken. He tried to sit up, but the ground beneath him shifted. He heard the clatter of dry bones. He tried to stand, but the bones shifted and he fell abruptly among them. Bani shivered. A spiral of cold pushed through his stomach to the top of his head. He rose and studied the contents of this crack in the earth.

Bani moved the branches that he had taken with him in his fall. He uncovered the bones of bears and people. Some bones were small, like the fragile skeleton of a newborn cub. The trap had been carefully reconstructed after the victims had come to rest on this cave floor. The mystery was when, and by whom, the trap was set. Bani felt along the walls for a foothold. He thought of the nimble goats that scale the vertical walls between the mountains, leaping from side to side on their magical hooves. Here the walls were too far apart for him to span with his body, and when he tried to grasp a jutting stone from the wall, it crumbled in his hand.

An unfamiliar mass was growing in his throat. It could not be long before it would explode and fill Bani with terror and despair. An odor, powerful enough to overwhelm the smell of old bones and dust, issued like a signal of distress from Bani's body. He tried to swallow the fear, but it grew big and filled the trap like smoke.

Suddenly, dirt and rocks rained down on him and his inert companions. He flung his arms over his head and tried to look toward the clamor above him. It was no human digging frantically at the edge of the trap. His throat burst. "Wolf!"

The animal worked furiously at the rim, its tail curved between its hind legs, its teeth clattering in concentration. Dirt flew through the air and down the sides, almost taking the young wolf with it. Bani, despite his dread, felt almost cheered at the wolf's valiant attempt to make the land level with the bottom of the cave. Perhaps sensing the futility of its actions, the wolf sat, raised its muzzle to the sky, and howled. *Who does he call,* thought Bani. Only the dead, with whom Bani now intimately huddled, could hear, but they were as helpless as he to ascend from this pitiless grave. Bani, calmer now that he was not alone, began to pile the bones against the wall in an attempt to climb upward. In his agitated state, he did not notice that the wolf had slipped away. "Wolf?" he said. But he was quite alone. The high noon sun cast a shaft of light alive with dust. As it narrowed and shifted its angle of penetration, he felt the darkness of death winding around him. He lay on the floor where he had cleared some bones, put his head down on his folded arms, and cried.

Xur circled the camp. He sniffed the late-afternoon air. Esur cast his eyes in his direction, but Xur avoided meeting his glance. He shivered. The cold touched him in unfamiliar ways. He approached the fire, but the flames licked at his hands like frost. He peered in the direction that Bani had taken, but the sky there was fading. The timbre of the wind against the bare trees scratched against his ears. From a long distance, he thought he heard Bani's flute. He concentrated all his attention toward the sound. *A wolf,* he thought, *a wolf singing down the sun.*

Bani's tears were spent, and without even meaning to, he began to think of a way to save himself. *What would Xur do in my place?* He swiped at his tears with a grubby forearm. Bani did not know enough to be afraid of the contents of that burial cave. He could not have noticed the arrangement of bones, laid out by the people who brought them there to tell a story. Large, human skeletons cradled small ones in the obtuse angle of an inflexible elbow, and in a posture of protection, a bear lay on its side, its rib cage large enough to contain all the other bones. Bani scattered this tableau when he fell and disturbed them further when he tried to clamor up the wall.

Bani, more carefully now, stacked the bones on one side of the cave. He worked through the afternoon, saving his flint to start a fire only when the afternoon light dissipated. He removed pieces of the crumbling wall to build a sloped base, tamping the dirt down so that it would not collapse when he was ready to climb. He removed only small, already loosened pieces so that the walls would not collapse on him and bury him alive. Sometimes he heard what he thought were footsteps, and he would cry out, "It's me, Bani. I'm down here." But no one was there. He continued to build; he even whistled and sang, refusing to lose hope. Then he lit a very small fire, pulled the last of his food from his pack, and thanked the spirits that dwelled under the skin of the earth for allowing him to visit for a while. He curled into himself, the ground warm and comforting, the small fire glowing, and dozed.

He woke later, the fire gone out, his heart hurting with the effort to keep it from beating too hard. The moon's light was indiscernible from the bottom of the pit. Not even a star glimmered through the leaf-obscured opening. No winter star for him to ponder, Bani countered his fear and started to work on his shaky platform, this time feeling his way through the darkness. He determined to work until morning. How many hours passed he could not tell, but the sun did rise and he could see the result of his night's work. When he fell, the bottom of the pit was three times as deep as Bani was tall. Since then, Bani had managed to construct a slope almost as high as he was. He was desperately hungry now, and in the dark, both his flint and his pack were buried in the sliding pile of rocks and loose dirt. He climbed to the top of the pile and sat down. He looked through the opening above him and tried to think of a quicker way to get out of there. The dirt shifted, and he slid a little way farther down. He tried to calculate the time he needed to repair this wound in the earth. He ran his hands over the crumbling walls, trying to discern an answer. He could feel a faint tremor in the ground. Despite the trickling dirt and rocks, he pressed his ear to the wall. *Not a man*, he said to himself, as the pounding grew louder.

Something on four legs was getting closer. Bani looked up expectantly. *Maybe an elk will fall down, and I can climb up on its antlers*, thought Bani. *Maybe a horse will come by, and I can make a rope of its tail.* He chuckled to himself, then stopped.

Maybe my bones will mingle with those scattered at the bottom of this pit.

He grabbed on to a jutting rock that came loose in his hand, then plunged farther down his handmade embankment. He stood, trying to regain his balance, when he heard the yip, yip of the wolf. He would have leaped in delight if he was on solid ground, but instead, he shouted an ecstatic greeting and waved his arms. The wolf peered over the edge, flung some dirt down on Bani's laughing face, then was gone.

"Come back. Come back. Please come back!"

Bani was stunned that the wolf appeared and then just as suddenly disappeared. He shouted uncontrollably. "Wolf." His throat rasped and his voice tore. "Wolf!"

"Bani, where are you?"

"I'm right here," he answered, believing in his excitement that it was the wolf that spoke.

"Bani, let me hear your voice so I can find you," said Xur.

Relief swept over him. "I fell into a trap, Xur, and I can't get out."

Xur leaned over the rim. "This is a very deep hole, Bani."

"I know," said Bani, "I'm trying to fill it."

"By throwing yourself in?" asked Xur, and the absurdity of Bani's situation struck them as very funny. "Wait there," teased Xur, and then they laughed until their eyes watered. Xur tossed Bani a small pouch of food and set about felling a birch. When he finished, he lowered the trunk into the pit and Bani scurried up as effortlessly as a squirrel taunting a cat.

CHAPTER EIGHTEEN

RED

Xur stroked a lithe shaft of new-growth oak. He hummed with contentment, the dread that often weighed on his chest gone off to look for someone else. He anticipated the companionship of the spear that waited beneath the delicate green leaves and gray-brown bark. The sea was a distant line on the horizon. He inhaled the metallic odor of salt, the tang of thawed grass, and the heady rot of mushrooms. The air promised nourishment. His outgoing breath ruffled the leaves. But before he could breathe in again, he sensed he was not alone.

What was that? The growl of a grizzly? Not deep enough. The howl of a wolf? Not high enough. Hyena? Not raucous enough. No lion would signal his intent to pounce. Animal or spirit, he picked up his weapon and moved toward the sound. It came from a thicket of low bushes that shook and swayed more violently as the cries grew louder. *What grieving woody spirit is this?* Xur gripped his spear. The thorny leaves sobbed and howled. "Help," a man's voice cried. Had the trembling bush consumed a man?

Xur moved closer. He called out, "Who is there?"

The cries abruptly ceased. The bush was still. The voice said calmly, "I am Red."

Red was a word used to describe the poisonous berries that grew on the bush. It was also the word for blood. He knew he shouldn't approach, but his legs carried him closer.

"Are you a man?" Xur asked. The bush let out a pitiful wail and shuddered. "I was . . . I was." And then Xur saw him.

Trussed like a corpse ready for burial, his legs drawn tightly against his chest, his crossed arms bound and clenched, Red was tied into a compact bundle.

"Ho," Xur cried out. "Are you dead?"

"I don't know," replied the man, sobbing so loudly that the sound thumped in Xur's chest. Xur put his weapon down and lifted Red's body from the bush. He was blood-smeared and bruised, but his head and limbs were intact. He placed him on the sandy clearing. He cut the ropes, and Red peered down his body in amazement and remained in the same position in which he was tied.

"Can you move your arms and legs?" Xur asked. Red shook his head. Xur studied Red's face as he massaged the places where he had been bound. Red howled in pain. "I am sorry to hurt you," said Xur. He wondered why a man—he decided that's what he was—should cry like a baby. Red's face was bearded, and he was close in age and size to Xur, although thicker through his neck and shoulders. Xur looked into Red's face, then took a quick step back. Red's forehead was a concave bowl under which his red, runny eyes sat as far apart as a frog's. His nose was flat and broad, as if his features were made of clay and someone or something had pushed hard against them and let them harden. Xur gently straightened the crying man's arms and legs. He lifted the man's head and gave him some water to drink.

"Can you stand?" Xur grasped Red under his arms and lifted him to his feet.

Red sat down again. "I'm tired," he said, frowning.

"Stay or go," said Xur, and he walked back to pick up his robe and tools. He cast a longing glance at the oak before heading east. He heard Red's footsteps behind him but he didn't look back. *Someone tied a tidy knot and left this bearded baby to die.* He did not want to learn the reason why.

Xur entered the camp and greeted everyone with his head down.

"What's wrong, Xur?" Mina asked. Before Xur could answer, the sound of Red trampling the dry bushes focused their attention. When he appeared, all adults reached for their weapons and pulled the children behind them. Xur said that he found Red and freed him and that he let Red come to camp with him just as he would any stranger.

"So here he is," Xur said.

Red listened as if he were not the object of Xur's explanation, his face expectant, innocent, and fixed. Xur didn't mention his initial fear or describe the sobs that revealed the profound weakness belying the robust, adult body.

Mina noticed the shiny scar on Red's ankle. Soon everyone was staring at the same spot. Red looked down at his own ankle, as curious as the rest.

Nin finally asked, "What are we looking at, Mother?"

"Red," said Mina, "what is your clan?"

Red looked confused.

"Where is your clan mark?"

"They took it off."

"Who took if off?"

"I don't remember," said Red, tears wetting his beard.

"Do you remember your clan name?"

"Yes."

"What is it?"

He pointed south. "The Mari."

Mina said, "Don't you mean north, Red?"

"Yes, north," he nodded.

"Did the Mari remove your mark?"

"My father did," said Red.

"Ho." Their breath whistled in shock.

Esur finally spoke, "Sit with us."

Red sat and ate the acorns, chicory, and raccoon, a little less for everyone now. He soon curled up very much the way Xur found him in the bush, except now, all cares were erased from his flat face. Snores fluttered through his soft lips, while the others looked at him and then at each other. It wasn't that Red looked different. How many times had they encountered men and women who survived disfiguring accidents or fights: limbs hacked off, faces scarred, eyes or ears lost through infection, ripped scalps where hair didn't grow or grew in patches, and the worst assault to defenseless flesh—fire. Xur could not imagine exile for the misfortune of being ugly. Then he felt bad for thinking of Red as ugly. But the Mari wanted to make sure he would not find his way back to them, even in death, and left him to be consumed in the harsh mountains of the Huul.

"Father." Xur started to say something, then stopped. They had taken in Blue, a stranger from much farther north than the Mari, and he had fed an attacking lion his hand in exchange for their lives. It was the rule that the people of the Huul and the neighboring clans always upheld: a stranger must be welcomed as if he were your own blood.

"Tomorrow, son," said Esur, and closed his eyes. But Xur knew that he did not sleep.

In the morning, Red was the last to awaken. Once again, food was shared. Rosh's son, Little Rosh, complained that he was still hungry while looking pointedly at Red, but he forgot soon enough when a hunt was planned and he was allowed to go along. Red stayed at the camp with Rosh's pregnant wife, Zu, along with Mina and the younger children.

Rosh's wife, flat on her back with her knees raised, watched the baby inside her body also search for a comfortable place to rest. During the morning, Red wandered off and was gone until noon. When he reappeared, he was carrying an enormous bundle of sharp-tasting greens.

"Thank you, Red," said the women.

Red ran off again, returning with branches and leaves, ripped haphazardly from the trees with his rough hands. "What should I do with these," asked Mina, but Red looked like he was about to burst into tears again, so instead, she handed him her axe. He took it and left.

The sun was traveling west, and the men and boys would be returning soon. Mina built up the cooking fire using a cache of dry wood. The leaves and buds and frayed green branches that Red contributed were thrown outside the camp, unsuitable for the hearth. "Forgive me, Mother, for tearing your limbs," Mina said.

"How long do you think Red will be among us?" asked Zu.

Mina sat down next to her and placed her right hand on Zu's rippling stomach.

"Do you think it will be tomorrow?"

"The baby coming or Red leaving," said Mina.

"Both, I hope," said Zu.

Just then, a hare bolted into the circle and right behind came Red, who hurled himself upon the creature. Red sprang up and held the stunned animal in one hand, knocking it on its head with the axe. He threw it to Mina, who was startled not only by the speed of the kill, but also by the dazzling, and toothless, smile on Red's face. Off he went again, hearing the returning party, impatient to tell Esur and Xur, Rosh and Blue, and his new young friends about his contribution to the meal, a tough, but tasty long-limbed hare. After eating, Red fell immediately asleep, splayed like a child exhausted by play.

The next day, Zu had a girl, and the NesGras family celebrated the mother and child. Red seemed as happy as they. He played with Bani, Nin, and little Blue, who spoke a few NesGras words and a few of his father's, too. Rosh's son, younger than Bani and Nin and not as grounded in the courtesies, grumbled when Red took the first and last bites of food, but he was stared down by his parents when his grumbling got too loud. Hyssop, always friendly and affectionate, was curious about their new company and ignored the disharmony rippling beneath the surface of courtesy and generosity. She was a child; Red only behaved as one.

"What happened to your face?" Mina asked.

Red put the greenstone he was trying to shape on the ground beside him. His eyes started to well. "I was hurt."

"Who hurt you?" Mina asked.

"A horse."

"How did the horse hurt you?"

"He stepped on me," said Red, and tears fell straight down his face and glistened in his beard.

Hyssop, watching over her new sister nearby, came over and touched Red's forehead.

"The hoof left a mark there," she said.

Red roared and hit the ground in front of them with his fist. "I hate that horse!"

Hyssop's short legs gave out, and she dropped to the ground with a startled laugh. "You hate a horse?"

Mina stood up. She wore her *do what I say right now* look. She needed, she said, Hyssop's immediate help on the other side of the camp to separate the earthnuts for their next meal.

"Mina, you're squeezing my arm," she said, as Mina pulled her up and away from the distraught man. "And I want to hear the story about the horse."

"Later," said Mina.

Another day passed, and for every hare or hen that Red brought to them, he ate two.

Nin and Bani, the same age and close in size, practiced their wrestling skills every day, although Red's interference began to dampen their enthusiasm. They were older now, and their simple grappling became more tactical. Rules were made up, refined, discarded, and replaced by new ones. The matches they saw at the meeting of the Huul had galvanized them, and they gauged their skill and strength against the one ideal they knew—Xur's match against Zuya.

Nin placed his left palm on Bani's right shoulder and pushed hard. When Bani reached across the inside of Nin's arm, Nin grabbed Bani's head and thrust one foot nimbly between Bani's feet, flipping him onto his back on the ground. "Show me how you did that," said Bani, and the boys reversed their roles, taking turns pressing their weight against each other's shoulder, until one lost his balance and the winner covered him on the ground. No one noticed that Red stepped to where the boys were playing, and before Bani could get up and grapple Nin, Red lifted Nin over his head and threw him to the ground. Nin lay there for a moment, eyes very wide, not moving. When he could breathe again, he got up, anger distorting his face. He head-butted Red in the stomach. Red, unmoved by the boy's retaliation, raised his fist, as Xur, running faster than anyone had ever seen him run, got to Red and shoved him, sending the larger man sprawling to the ground.

"I was playing!" he said.

"You cannot play with children," Xur said. Red sat on the ground with his legs straight out in front of him and folded himself over so that his head touched his knees. Xur, feeling like he was the bully, said more softly, "You are not a child."

Yet, the simple rules of childhood games eluded him. And what was worse, he knew that he could never learn them.

Everyone in the camp—women, babies slung on their backs, older children, and the men—went to the marshy coast to gather reeds and frogs, mallow and voles. They collected shells as big as platters and as small as fingernails. Hunters could pick off the birds that gathered in great staring rows along the inlets, intent on the flitting fish below their sharp bills.

Esur lagged behind, his joints stiff and sore in the dampness. The small children walked at their own pace, running as crookedly as rabbits. Zu carried her newborn and was the last in the column of travelers. When they all arrived, Zu sat on a fallen log and prepared to nurse the baby. The day was cool and mild. Wind ruffled the feathers of the otherwise still birds and gently stippled the surface of the marsh.

Red wandered back to where the women were sitting. He held a duck by one webbed foot, its broken neck lolling close to the ground. He dropped the duck and picked up an unfinished hammerstone. Nearby, the three young children played in a circle, Little Blue running in raucous delight on his short, firm legs. Hyssop, Bani's age, was no taller than her younger brother, Little Rosh. They ran squealing, chasing each other, throwing mud and sticks. Red moved closer to them. The children's noise grew louder, and the birds fluttered away from their perch. Esur pulled himself up to quiet the children. Red put his hammerstone down. Esur didn't try to outshout them as he limped toward them. Hyssop, still laughing, ran away from Esur toward Red and picked up his hammerstone. She jumped crookedly up and down in front of him, making sure he could see she had his treasure, knowing that he, just as any boy, would take up the chase. She laughed hard. Red ran after her. Esur was close now. Rosh's wife screamed, "Stop. Hyssop, put it down. Stop!" Red launched himself and landed hard on top of Hyssop, grinding her into the packed dirt, butting the back of her small head with his flat forehead. The lopsided stone tumbled from her hand. Red jumped to his feet and picked up the stone. He lifted his arms above his head as if claiming a great victory. Esur ran toward Hyssop. Her mother's screams alarmed all the birds, which took off in one great whoosh.

"I didn't do it," said Red. Mina and the others ran to where Hyssop lie. Rosh's wife could not be constrained from lifting her. Mina sponged away the blood that seeped from the child's nose, ears, and mouth. Her eyes were open, as if she was surprised by the sudden tumble, then they closed in a rapid descent into sleep. The blood stopped only in the morning when her spirit joined the wind. Her mother wailed, and her father pushed his fists into his temples. Red scuttled to the edge of the treeline. "I didn't do it," he said.

Hyssop was shrouded in the soft, tan robe that was her first garment. Her father made her a necklace from the smallest shells, painted with ochre and strung on twine. Bani placed a stone with the face of a flower in her hand and closed her fingers around it. Her mother wrapped her feet with hide to protect her from the hard ground. She sleeps, they said, as they swaddled her in strips of fur to keep her warm and secure. They placed her deep within a cave and sealed the entrance. The nightfires were lit. Esur looked at Rosh, who nodded in response. Red hid beyond the edge of their camp. "I didn't do it," they could hear him say.

"Tomorrow," said Esur.

In the morning, Red cringed as Rosh and Esur approached him. "We will hunt today," they said.

Red, as if born anew, jumped to his feet. "I don't have a spear," he said.

"I have two," said Esur, as they disappeared together down a slippery path west.

CHAPTER NINETEEN

NAKI SWIMS

Naki ran to where the sand was dry. He dropped his tools and tossed off his clothes, leaving only two thin strands of beads and shells around his neck. Sura pulled her wrap tighter. Her lower legs and feet were numb to where the water teased and ebbed. Naki splashed past her. They had been walking along the shore, side by side, wading to where the sea dissolved into foam, looking for holes in the wet sand where crabs took their tiny breaths. Now that it was getting toward sunset, the waves rose higher and broke closer in before scurrying back to the glowing horizon.

That morning, when they came to gather mussels from the broken rocks that sprang from the ocean, the sun was warm. They kept dry and filled up on the salty, orange membranes that adhere inside the hard, glossy shells. Naki was already too far out to hear when he plunged into a wall of water as it swelled and crested above his head. Sura stumbled backward, crying out his name. The waves charged and crashed before rushing back to the deeper ocean, as if gathering angry courage for another assault on the shore. Never had Sura seen anyone go to where the sea was a darker blue than the sky.

Like a baby tossed into the air, Naki trusted the sea to catch him. It was green where she stood amid the thick-leaved, floating plants, green from the muckish beard of the mussels and the bright-green moss that covered the rocks. A sucking vortex drained the sand under her, and pebbles sharp as stony blades rushed in to pull her out to sea by her feet. Sura's heart pounded. All she could see of Naki was his swimmer's arms, arcing through the rising and falling ocean until he disappeared into another high wave, sometimes glimmering through like an insect caught in amber. She scrambled to get upright and only succeeded in falling and getting dragged in deeper. She opened her mouth to call out, and the intense saltiness and graininess of the sea overwhelmed her.

Naki rode in on a wave beside her, rotating his arms against the undertow and moving his body like a frog. He grabbed her arm and pulled her to the lapping, puddling shore. Her eyes and throat stung, and she threw up the water she had swallowed and most of the half-digested mussels she had eaten. He was breathing hard. And laughing! Broken shells glittered in his hair. His wet skin was pebbled from the cold. Black hair that had thickened this last year grew into a pattern that was the shape of his body—broad across his chest, narrow down his belly, heavy around his groin, and covering his arms and legs like a loosely woven cloak, black hair that stood on end from the cold. He didn't notice. She shuddered. A rising wind made her wet clothes feel like she was encased in ice. The angling sun was big and bright but no longer warmed them. Naki tugged on her cape.

"Take off your clothes, Sura."

"I thought you drowned, Naki."

He helped her up, and they walked to where his clothes still lay. He put hers next to his on the dry sand. She shivered, and Naki picked up his blanket and wrapped it around her. Her lips brushed his shoulder. She tasted his skin. Brine and fish and sand. A clean taste. His hand went to the back of her neck, his fingers through her hair. He pulled her close to him. His other hand warmed her back, supporting her, cradling her as they sunk to the sand, and the blanket fell open like a ripe blossom beneath them. Naki's heat filled her. She held him, and the green iris of the sea watched. They were together there until the sea became jealous and crept up to where their naked feet flouted its power, and they rose to tread their way back under a starless, cerulean sky. Naki gave Sura his dry clothes to wear, and he faced the wind and coming cold like long anticipated friends who would bring him gifts.

CHAPTER TWENTY

BANI'S STARS

Two almost seasonless years of abundance had passed since Sura joined the Nir. Spears of cereal grass bowed down under their own weight, tender under a summer sky that held an enormous red sun at the end of the day. Mallow was crushed under a stone, boiled, and eaten throughout its season and beyond. The cooing mouth of the full moon kissed the reflecting water and kept it calm. Two winters without snow—only rain swelled the streams and diluted the salt of the southern lake.

Xur brought Juul to live with them, a Willow like his own mother, shy under Xur's gaze. Little Blue was strong and healthy, a fortunate blend of Mina's brown earth and his father's gray sky. Blue used what remained of his right arm with almost as much dexterity as his missing fingers, manipulating and balancing his flute with his left, and using his recovered knife as if he had prepared for the loss all along.

Bani lay on his back and held his arms straight up. He spread his fingers against the sky. Tonight, the moon was a narrow silhouette, hiding its face from the spectacle of light. How many fires burned there? Who rekindled them after a heavy rain? Why were they brightest on the coldest nights? Where did they go in the daytime? He spread his fingers so that each fingertip touched a star, measuring it against his own smallness.

He put both hands into the soot of a spent campfire and ran to the far wall inside the cave. The torch he lit and set in the entry emitted thick smoke and smelled of grease. Bani didn't notice. He pressed his blackened hands to the wall until the imprints receded, waving to him in the flickering light. He regarded his work. What was missing from his panorama? He filled his mouth with the charred remains of firewood and pressed his palm against the wall. He sprayed the wet charcoal mist over his hand, leaving a black outline when he removed it. *Yes*. He did it again. Negative and positive images crowded the rough wall, as high and as low as he could reach, into the blind, unlit shadows beyond the torchlight. The uncountable stars swept and tumbled across the stony sky. He ran outside.

"What are you doing, Bani?" asked Nin.

"There are so many lights in the sky."

"There are," said Nin without looking up.

"Have you ever wondered at the abundance of them, or why we have never come across those that have lit the fires, or why some travel, then go out, or why they seem no closer, even from the top of the tallest mountains?"

Nin did not bother to look at the mountains or the stars that crowded the night sky. "No," he said and went inside. Sometime later, he strolled out and sighed.

"Bani, what is that on the wall?"

Bani showed Nin his blackened hands.

"Why have you wiped your hands on the wall?"

"Because of the stars," he said, as if explaining it all.

Nin finally looked up. The sky looked the same as it always did, reminding him that it was time to go to sleep and to stay as close to his mother's campfire as he was allowed. *Because of the stars*, Nin repeated to himself and sighed again. He wrapped his sleeping robe tightly around him, nestled his head on his folded arms, and fell immediately to sleep.

Bani did not sleep. Was he foolish? He did not know himself the point of his effort, a wall with countless handprints. Does anyone else see stars the way he saw them? Do the ancestors stoke the fires as a light for the living? What is fire for? To keep predators at bay, to cook food and keep you warm. Fire hardened the sharp tips of tools and weapons and softened and cured blankets and clothing. They saw each other's faces across the fire and told stories. They carried fire when they could and used sparks left behind by lightning to set new blazes. They extracted fire from moss and dry wood. But who were the makers of fire that burned beyond their reach and what were their stories?

Bani knew that an overabundance of curiosity was not only use-less, it was also dangerous and arrogant. An adult must be able to read the directions and seasons from the patterns above them. One's eyes were to be trained on the ground they walked on, the search for food the overriding activity. He shut his eyes but could still see the glimmer of light. Seven bright stars settled in the west, low on the jagged, black horizon, the bones of the earth rigid in sleep.

Bani heard women singing. He rose from his bed to move closer to the voices. His floated just above the ground. It seemed the most sensible way to walk. The sky was so much closer now, but he still could not see who lit those limitless fires. He rose too high and was afraid. There was no up or down. He started to tumble, and the terror startled him. The stars were far away. Was he still dreaming? The constellations, the wolf, the bear, the tree that bifurcated north and south, east and west, glowed and winked. The canopy of lights held a message. The trail of smoke that tumbled across a great expanse, the path the dead took, beckoned him and he was not afraid.

A few days' walk away from where Bani dreamt, Sura regarded the same stars. She pressed close to Naki, and above them, the trail of smoke covered them like a blanket.

The Nir flourished under the warming sun. Tehil and Zamia would be with her when her child was born. And Naki's brother Dzo added to the clan with a new wife from the Wolf Moon clan who laughed and told stories. The growing season lasted longer, nourishing the people of the clans and other creatures along with them. Life teemed and tangled like twine that strengthened with each added strand, resilient until cut by a blade or snapped by tension.

CHAPTER TWENTY-ONE

A CHILD IS WAITING

Sura dozed, her eyes not completely shut, aware of both her dreams and the agreeable murmurs around her. She was awake enough to know if Alu, who got angry with anyone who rested in her presence, wanted something or someone. Alu, yellow eyes like pebbles in a pouch, seemed as old as her father, both still driving the Nir—Tell by teaching what he knew, and Alu by tantalizing everyone with her secrets and spells of menacing silence.

Sura's stomach was a small, hard mound under her shift, beginning to quicken with life. In her reverie, an infant, just old enough to sit up in that straight-spined way infants have before they can stand alone, spoke to her. She listened, amazed that a baby that young could speak. She couldn't make out what it said, but the baby laughed as it spoke. Sura nestled into the dream, enjoying the imagined company more than the real people around her, the old, who had an excuse to snore with their chins buried in their chests, popping awake occasionally to shout a comment, and the very young, who rested their heads in their parents' laps and let their eyes lose focus and drift, seeing clouds turn into aurochs and mammoths. Sura's languor let her escape from the ceremony that had buzzed and droned since dawn, and the voices dissipated on the mild, spring air.

"This Nir woman chooses to become a Wolf Moon and live with them, share their food and fire, and walk beside this man"—the speaker pointed to someone smothered under layers of clothing and strings of beads and painted shells—"called Tav by his Wolf Moon mother and his Wolf Moon father." Sura could barely stand to hear the words *Wolf Moon* again.

When she and Naki had been promised to each other, she had been so stiff and frightened that she hadn't heard anything anyone said. A good thing, or she would have run back to the less ceremonious NesGras. After two years with the Nir, she was accustomed to their love of ritual, of repetition, which the entranced Nir seemed never to get enough. She chuckled to herself. Now that everyone knew she was pregnant, her intense sleepiness was a source of amusement to the Nir relatives, except for Alu, who didn't sleep at all. Instead, she fell into a trance that no one could disturb. If Alu watchers were amused, they didn't show it. What would have seemed like strange behavior in someone else was held sacred in her. Even the most active gossipers in the Nir camp pressed their lips together and studied the ground when Alu passed.

What did the talking infant say, Sur wondered. Nothing about the outstanding qualities of the Wolf Moon man who sat looking as stricken as the equally smothered Zamia, the center of attention and the reason for the forthcoming feast. Yes, he chose her and she chose him, and their parents were filled with joy. Except Zamia's parents were dead. Alu had raised her, and Manul had no interest in children, unless, like Fox, they prematurely bloomed into womanly form.

Was the infant a good sign? Was it a warning? She was afraid to ask Alu, and Mina and her NesGras family were not here. Sura didn't expect them this year. Naki was oblivious to her questions, looking up from his tools and shells, bones and beads, nodding his head, concentrating on the work of his hands. Tehil might know, but Sura suspected that Tehil looked at her many questions as a NesGras peculiarity, a trait that tested and challenged powerful forces that should not be disturbed.

All morning they cooked. Spring deer and gazelle hung suspended over the fire, and surf-ridged clamshells caught dripping fat that was rubbed over the brown meat by hands that were inured to the heat and flames. Hours before, the promised ones, Zamia and the Wolf Moon man, ate the raw, glistening livers, blood smooth and sumptuous. All of it. No wonder they sat so still. The fat in their guts must have weighed them to the ground.

Sura was hungry. She wished for duck liver, red and rich, warm and alive. Or the heart. Thinking of the tender ducks that would come soon, she took out the ball of fat, dried meat, berries, and nuts she carried with her, the last of a winter store made from summer's bounty. She took a bite without opening her eyes. She chewed slowly. The roasting meat scented the air and made the dried tack, which could be eaten years after it was made, taste even worse. She swallowed the dry concoction and stuck her tongue out to find out if she could taste the meat in the air and erase the bitterness from her palate. Naki nudged her. Sura sat up, stretched her legs out in front of her, and crossed her ankles like a proper Nir woman. She pressed her arm against Naki's, and he leaned closer into her. Sura felt warm. Even the rain, which seemed to caress rather than chill her, did not disturb her quietude and satisfaction.

Zamia sat in the middle of the circle of people—Wolf Moon and Nir, Willow and NesGras. Next to her was the Wolf Moon. *Just a boy*, Sura thought. She had seen him playing with Nin and Bani only the year before. *Could that be?* As long as no one jostled her or expected her to reply, she was content to wander in her own thoughts of talking babies and Wolf Moon boys who came from the southern hills looking for Nir girls to bring back with them.

Alu was busy with the rituals and preparations. "I'll finally be rid of that foolish girl," she said. Sura and Tehil suspected that Zamia, who had been sheltered by Alu since her mother had died, meant more to her than one less body around the fire. Before the planning for this ceremony started, Alu had spent a great deal of time by herself, coming back with her fingernails broken and black from digging in the soil around the western shore of the freshwater sea. It was not Nir land. It was Willow land, or too close to Willow land for Alu to be gathering her seeds and herbs, and no one knew what else, to concoct no one knew what, and bury it no one knew where.

Zamia's coming year would be used to prepare her for her role as a Wolf Moon. Tehil's intended husband was dead, killed by what the Nir called a wandering spear. Tehil, truly her mother's daughter, did not weep and snapped at Zamia when she asked, "No, he has no brothers."

The rain was falling harder now, muddying the ground across the camp. Smoke blew black and thick, and warming fires were being built closer to the sheltering rock walls and under branches. Sura sprang up, forgetting to be tired, eager to help Zamia wash away some of the ochre and charcoal that Sura knew stung her eyes and made her head itch where it caked in her scalp. She shared a meal with Naki, then the men gravitated toward the center of the camp. The women gathered around Zamia, combing the yellow pigment from her hair, undoing braids and removing the beads, washing her all over with the fallen rain that was cached and warmed in iridescent shells big enough to take two hands to carry, brimming with scented liquid.

Zamia started to cry, her eyes already very red from the ground clay that leaked into them, and her nose ran. Finally, she sobbed. "Sura," she said, "I don't want to die."

The women clucked over her. "Die? Only your fears will die, Zamia." But Sura knew what they all knew. When a woman left her kin to travel with another, she did not come back.

"It will be a long time before you leave us," said Sura, "and our paths will cross many times even after you are a Wolf Moon." But all the while she spoke reassuringly to Zamia, she thought of Mina and her father and brothers, and her heart remembered the ache when she separated from her family.

"Am I to finish this feast alone?" Alu broke in. "Why are you crying, Zamia? Do you think you are still sitting in the place of honor with that green stick-boy?"

Zamia stopped whimpering. "No, Mother, there is dust in my eyes."

"There will be more than dust in your eyes if you don't stop complaining." And even though no one knew exactly what Alu meant, her threat was enough for Zamia to sit still and for the other women to stop comforting her and complete cleaning her face. *Green stick-boy*, thought Sura. *That will be his name forever.*

The next day, Sura, Zamia, and Tehil followed Alu along the path that took them to the Great Meeting.

"Why are we going back, Alu?" Tehil's sour look made her resemble her mother more than ever.

Zamia and Sura held hands and walked close behind the mother and daughter, struggling to match their pace. Tehil was now taller than her mother, her legs longer, shoulders and hips broader. She seemed to hold herself more erect than the other young Nir woman. She was aloof now, smiling less than the days when the three girls formed a bond against the fearsome demands of Alu.

Sura never spoke of her relief that Tehil would stay with the Nir and continue to be her companion. She knew that such selfish thoughts must be wiped from her mind. After all, a young man died. But Tehil had started to withdraw before his death, growing sharp in conversation and avoiding the company of the other women of the camp who took up what they felt was Alu's lack of commitment in finding a mate for her daughter. Not that they criticized Alu directly. They just insinuated that, unlike her mother, Tehil couldn't live in the camp of her father without creating a rift in the natural balance of things.

"We're passing barley," Zamia said, but Alu didn't even turn her head. A goat trotted in and out of the shadows, and a kid skittered on the rocks close behind her. Still Alu advanced. The sun was level with their shoulders. The rain, fine as smoke and as light as dew, started and stopped at the urging of a mild wind.

"Here," said Alu, and they all paused at the place they had stayed only weeks before. Rocks smoothed by a steady stream of runoff glistened. The soil on either side, dry when they were there last, was moist, and green shoots covered an area as big as a campsite that would be used for three or four people. In fact, it was a campsite used by three people—Alu, Zamia, and Tehil—and it was there that Alu spilled her store of hard seeds, tediously separated from the spears of wheat that grew in sparse tufts along the river and around the northern lake. Here they grew in clusters, green in the wet soil, huddling against each other as if in protection from the grim wind that, in this mildest of springs, failed to display its power.

Alu took her blade and cut a handful of green shoots. "Taste."

The young women chewed. "It is good," said Tehil, "but why did we have to walk so far? We passed many things we could eat."

Zamia and Sura waited for Alu to say something sharp or to grab the shoots back, but instead, she laughed. "Sura, tell me what is different about this food."

Sura bent down and pulled some of the shoots from the ground. "No!" Alu said. "Cut them the way I did. Do you think they will continue to grow if you pull out their roots?"

Sura knew that the tough wheat grew back in the places where it was pulled up. Everyone saw seeds scatter on the wind when they wrestled the plants from the ground. Undigested seeds in the droppings of animals sprouted on the surface of the ground. Now she saw that immature plants followed the damp contours of the stream, not randomly in the water or in the dry earth that sloped up to the foothills. No, the soft, new growth followed around the bend of the wet path as far as they could see. Alu had not carelessly spilled the seeds it would have taken to grow so many new plants clustered together. Hard seeds gleaned from gathered plants were stored for future use. Whenever mature wheat and barley plants were disturbed, the seeds scattered before the ice and cold killed them. But Alu did not merely return to a particularly fecund spot. She did something entirely new and different. She nurtured the seeds, prodded their growth. She dropped them, but not because she was careless. She placed them, as one would place an infant near the hearth to keep it warm, in a place she would be sure to find again.

"Where is she now?"

Sura came to a group of women talking in whispers. "She is not here."

"No one blames her."

"A coward?"

"Worse?"

Sura asked, "What are you talking about?"

"Don't you know?" a tall Wolf Moon woman asked.

"Know what?"

"About the NesGras woman."

"I am a NesGras woman," said Sura.

"You are a Nir"—Tehil and Zamia joined the group—"and your Nir sisters are here."

Sura sensed a warning.

Tehil and Zamia greeted the women. "Alu took us far today."

Tehil stopped speaking when the women's lips tightened at the mention of Alu's name. Men and women sang, and over that, the high-pitched screeches of excited children carried over to them. They had no need to whisper. Even if they shouted, no one even a short distance away could hear them.

"You'll learn this anyway when the rest of the travelers arrive, but a NesGras woman east of where your family lives, Sura, killed her child this winter."

"Why?" Sura was stunned.

"Not for sport," the oldest of the women answered. "A lion attacked. She hid, but her child was crying, so she held her hand over its face to keep it from making noise. You can imagine the rest."

"I can't imagine the rest," Sura said.

Tehil circled Sura's arm with her fingers before Sura could step toward the older woman. Sura tried to move her arm, but Tehil squeezed tighter.

"There are only two NesGras bands meeting us here. The woman's band is not among them."

"Where is your family, Sura?"

"Sura waits, as we all do," another of the women said.

Sura wasn't sure why she felt so angry with these women. What could she say that did not sound like caviling? My father is nearly bent in half from the disease that twists the spine like a winded oak, and the others will not abandon him. Mina's child is too young to walk and too large to carry the many miles over two mountain ranges. Rosh is mourning for his dead child. Sura believed that despite their reconciliation, there was still much distance between the two peoples. She knew what many said, that the NesGras were proud and stubborn in a way that was not only bad for themselves, but bad for others, too. That they still held a grudge against

Tell, and that they did believe his acts of sacrifice brought peace between the people and the buffeting winds of the Huul. Sura watched them tilt their faces toward the sun as if it were their right alone. *Pride is not only a fault found in the NesGras.* To the women, she said, "They will be here," and she felt the flush the lie brought to her face. Tehil loosened her grip, yet kept her hand in place. Sura felt as she often did among the Nir—comforted by the closeness of many people and constrained by the same hands that kept her in place among them.

The older woman continued. "This woman was not young, and the child was her only living child. Since you cannot imagine it, Sura," she said, "I tell you that fear makes us strong and fear makes us weak. We are like a herd of horses, frightened by a wave of cloth, running in panic, forgetting the foal that stumbles and becomes wolf's food. Don't think the mare doesn't pine for its young, whom she licked and nourished with her own milk, any less than this NesGras mother cherished her own child."

Sura felt Tehil's fingers tighten again. "Forgive me, Mother," Sura said. "I will remember what you've told me."

No year passed without the death of a child, or a weakened adult, by a lion. Hunters in the prime of speed and strength were devoured, their hard skulls and broken weapons left behind for the crushing power of hungry hyenas. To hear that rumble in the lion's throat, that clacking of great teeth, was to be driven mad with fear. And madness was either forgiven or diverted, unless the afflicted caused harm to the group. One child in abundant times was a sustainable loss, but for the dwindling NesGras living in their high mountain home, even one loss was hard.

The talking child appeared again that night, and when she reached for it, there was silence. Sura felt great sadness, as if she had lost a keepsake. Now the dead NesGras child was conflated with the talking child of her dream, and Sura was the mother who smothered its cries. She left the shelter and found that Naki had fallen asleep around the center hearth, where he and his brothers and cousins talked and ate themselves into exhaustion. Happy flies buzzed around the remains of the feast, and moths tempted the dying flame to consume them.

"Naki." She shook him and he was pleased to see her, oblivious of the fear that made her tremble despite the night being unseasonably warm. Naki half rose and wrapped his arms around her knees.

"Naki, have you heard about the NesGras mother?"

Naki smiled up into Sura's face. "No, tell me," he said, hugging her tighter so that Sura had trouble keeping her balance.

"About the NesGras mother who killed her child?"

Naki stood up, not happy with the direction this conversation was taking.

"Are you listening to those Wolf Moon women, Sura?"

"How can I not listen, Naki?"

"Did you know this woman and child?"

"No," said Sura.

"Was the child eaten by the lion?"

"It wasn't said."

"The child's spirit waits for its mother. Eaten or buried, it waits. Believe that, Sura."

And Sura let Naki wrap her in his arms as she stole a glance at the pulsing stars above her in the cold sky where a silent child waited for its mother.

CHAPTER TWENTY-TWO

ABUN

The Nir moved south, away from the shore, closer to the inland lake that provided plentiful food in any season. A warm, wet summer encouraged the oaks to produce copious amounts of acorns, the deer's favorite forage. They argued over which was more succulent, deer that grazed on acorns or gazelle on clover. The crescent of the Huul held summer in its curved grasp, reluctant to let in the shade of winter across the hills and valleys.

Alu had fashioned a pack for Sura to carry on her back. Her stomach was now in the way of seeing her feet, but it provided a handy ledge for her meal when she was sitting. Walking, it pulled her forward, heavy and dropping lower every day. Sura wanted to stop and relieve herself, and when she did, a viscous substance leaked out. She felt full, cramped, and aching across her back, and a sharp pain started below her low-slung stomach.

"I would like to sit down now," she said. She wasn't far from their camp, and besides Alu and her daughters, there were two other Nir women with them, all laden with acorns, barley, and the brittle wheat that shattered when they gathered it. What they didn't grind and eat would make the straw for bedding, insulation against the cooling ground. It was warm now, but winter would undoubtedly rouse itself from where it slept in the north.

Alu kept the seeds separate from each other—barley in one pouch, wheat in another, and ripe and bitter olives in yet another. If she was not Alu, they would have laughed and taken all the seeds together, placing them on the large, flat stone in the middle of their camp, grinding them with fat and berries, eating as they ground, and keeping the rest to store against the coming winter.

Sura sat down on the path. "I think he wants to leave me," she said.

Alu told Sura to lie down and peered between her legs. "Get up," she said. "We have time to get back."

Tehil and Zamia lifted a very reluctant Sura from the ground, took her burden of acorns, hooked their arms through hers, and supported her for the last miles back. "I'm sick," Sura said, and she threw up down the front of her shift. She felt very sorry for herself and for indifference the other women showed as they hurried her along. Alu walked ahead toward the hearth outside the hut that Naki had put up to shelter Sura while she gave birth. It was big enough for the three or four women who would stay with her until she could care for the infant by herself. Tehil and Zamia were almost carrying Sura now and with a final exertion got Sura inside. She noticed, as she sank down on the bedding, that a small pallet was on the ground beside her. Rather than the straw that they all used for insulation, the little bed was stuffed with down from a winter's worth of ducks. "Oh, Naki," Sura said, "you are such a clever man."

Tehil and Zamia kneeled on either side of her as the birthing pains became stronger. Alu, wearing only her shift, better to keep her strong arms unencumbered, was staring intently at the place where the baby would emerge. Sura could see the blazing hearth through the entry of the hut. The hides that covered the ceiling were turned back so that the sun, now directly overhead, lit the interior. In-between the pains, Sura said, "This

isn't so bad," but she screamed so loud when they struck that Zamia let go
of her hand and covered her ears. Sura thought for a moment that Naki
came to the doorway of the hut and was about to call out to him, but when
she focused, he was not there. Sura denied later that she had bellowed like
a wounded elk.

Tehil rolled her eyes. "Courage is not always silent," she said.

The sun was still high above them when Abun was born, ripping
the birth canal only enough for his round head to push its way through.
Sura could feel the quick stitches Alu made to close the wound once the
afterbirth was expelled. Sura would be strong enough before the sun set to
bury it, sustenance for the earth, substitute for Abun, whose life was safe
for at least a little while. His name would not be spoken aloud today. The
Nir did not dare tempt fate that boldly. But his small arms were round, and
his knees were dimples in his plump, ruddy flesh. He was lying just next to
her when she came back to herself, and when he turned his head, his black
eyes looked directly into Sura's, piercing her with overwhelming love. She
picked him up and placed his pliable, little body on her still soft but now
flat stomach. He fit there and tried to lift his head on his wobbly neck so he
could see the features of his mother just as she studied his new face. When
the effort to memorize each other's features exhausted them, mother and
child slept, warm and comfortable, and the red smell of blood was washed
away. The smells of lavender and willow took its place as Zamia and Tehil,
her sisters, bathed them both.

"Time to rise," Alu said. Sura didn't hesitate and got up silently, carrying her son against her breast. She went with the women and dug a narrow
grave in the place where the Nir buried their dead, interring the afterbirth
so the earth would have its share and be satisfied. The night was dark, cold,
and bracing, but when they got back to the birthing hut, the fire was warm.
Abun's only sound was a soft, milky burp and a sigh of contentment. Naki
waited for them there, looking giddy and stunned, and placed a cord with
a single, perfect, wooden bead around the infant's neck, lifting his son's

surprisingly heavy head, which pulsed slightly at the crown. Sura touched Abun's cheek and he turned toward her finger, his mouth searching, his eyes closed, trusting them to see for him. Tehil and Zamia came in and shooed Naki out. Through the hole at the top of the tent the smoke passed straight up, and all of the mothers' fires in the indigo sky burned bright.

CHAPTER TWENTY-THREE

TEHIL DOESN'T CRY

The gossipers, men and women, said because she had not thrown her body on his grave or drowned the stones with her tears, she wasn't unhappy enough. Tehil hadn't looked on anyone since her promised Wolf Moon man died. She didn't return to his clan and present herself with her eyes spilling charcoal down her cheeks. She didn't ask the expected questions. Whose young wife died in childbirth or a fall, or burned to a cinder in a cooking fire? Who had a lonely space by his campfire? Whose mother pressed a son to find a companion and bring her relief? Alu was silent. If she spoke to Tehil, guided her away from Tell's camp, no one's ears were pricked by the advice. Sura and Tehil were Alu's only companions on her forays into places where the most tender of grasses grew in abundance. Only they seemed to be able to find these places, and they remained silent.

The gossipers peered into Tehil's life like those small squirrels that stand up on their tiny hind legs when someone dropped a seed or two on the ground. No, Tehil did not look on anyone with favor since the young man died. A few remarked that she didn't seem to look on the poor dead boy with favor, either. She was not shy. Tehil didn't cast her eyes downward, as many girls did, pretending not to notice while signaling their interest and denying it at the same time.

Perhaps Tehil was like the women who shared their shelter with other women. Good for the orphans they sniffed, two women building a fire together, raising children who for one sad reason or another had no mother or father, grandparent or aunt to look after them. Everything worked out equitably that way. Yet, Tehil was getting old in the narrow society of women without mates. Not a widow, not an adolescent, just alone. She was tall like Alu, and she was like her mother in other ways. *Remember Alu's first husband, the wretched Two, they said, killed by hyenas, although no one in memory, living or otherwise, had heard of hyenas attacking and killing an adult.*

What animal killed Tehil's man?

Not an animal. The fire from his own mother's hearth consumed him.

No, that wasn't him.

I remember. A boulder no one could have moved alone rolled on him while he slept.

A tree. As he ate.

He fell off a high cliff into the sea.

Tehil told him he had to come live with Alu and the shame killed him.

I asked Naki what happened, and he shook his head at me. What do you think he meant by that?

They agreed on one thing: silence meant secrets—and a good story waiting to be told.

The truth was that Tehil's promised got wet on a cold night, lay down with a high fever, and died in full, teeth-chattering view of his entire clan. Tehil liked the young man. She wasn't like the weeping Zamia, afraid to leave her mother's fire. But he was dead, and she had no desire to replace him with another. No one would coerce her to leave the Nir. She knew what they said and what was expected of her. She simply lacked the talent for tears and dramatic cries of lamentation. She could stay an unmarried woman if she wanted. Isn't that what Alu did before Manul took pity on her? Stay with the Nir whose population burgeoned in good times and bad? A few more people, especially a woman like Tehil, would benefit them, and though her grandfather outlived trees that split rocks with their tenacious roots, his daughter Alu couldn't live forever. Of Tell's living descendants, who better than Alu could retrieve the reluctant newborn from the clamped womb or put the blood back into a broken body? And Tehil was so like her mother.

And look at Sura. We admire her intelligence and agility, and she keeps Alu's secrets so well. Her son, Abun, is so fat and mild, as if he took his strength from the weak children who did not survive the rigors of their own birth. As mine did not, they said. It's no wonder she dotes on him as if he was very special.

Zamia was gone. Sura and Tehil were left behind to lean against the wall of Nir chatter and the intransigence of Alu's bluster. Sura slept with Naki at night, but days brought the three women together, distant from the others.

"Tehil, you never speak about your Wolf Moon man."

"Man?" She snorted. "He was a boy. And now he's dead."

Sura stretched and pressed her hands against the small of her back. Abun was weaned and she was pregnant again, and this child was already weighing heavily against her spine.

"I'm sorry that he died."

Tehil cut a long stalk, careful not to shake the seeds loose.

"You know I'm pleased that you're here"—she waited for Tehil to answer her unasked question—"especially now that a new child will be born soon, should we live through winter," she added, feeling the pang of anxiety caused by her arrogance. A sudden, cold breeze snapped against them. Sura shuddered. Tehil's hair lifted and fell; every other part of her remained still. Her hand grasped a shaft of barley, and her back curved toward the black, damp earth. Sura didn't see Alu. She couldn't be sure that Alu heard them. She wanted to comfort Tehil, who no longer wore the ochre and charcoal that so fascinated Sura when she first saw the girls primping in their mother's shelter. Once a girl was mated, her face was left unadorned. Tehil was alone. Two winters had already passed since the death, yet she still did nothing to signal her intentions.

Sura tried again. "Is it my selfishness that keeps you?"

Tehil straightened and looked past her. Sura remembered the deer that froze in the bright flash of the storm, staring, blind from too much light. Sura tried to see what it was that Tehil saw when another blast of air unfurled their clothing like the wings of ascending gulls.

"Yes," said Tehil.

"I try not to be selfish," Sura said, surprised at Tehil's bluntness.

Tehil laughed for the first time in a long while. "No, it's a good thing. You know how to move alone. Another girl would have been too afraid to leave her brother's side. You chose the wrong path, but you never felt shame from your mistake, so you were forgiven. You trusted two men who were strangers to you and they honored your trust. And now you are a Nir . . . of a sort."

"Of a sort? I'm your sister, Tehil. Does Alu share this place with anyone but us, her daughters?"

Tehil pulled a young plant from the ground, moved an arm's length away, poked a hole in the dirt with her finger and placed the shoot gently in the hole, tamping the earth to keep the wind from blowing it away.

"This is you, Sura, plucked from one place and taking root in another. You say you would die if you were separated from Naki, but you would live. Your children will live. I see that."

"And you?" Sura said. "Do you see yourself taking root somewhere else or being alone?"

"I'm not alone. I have many Nir cousins who mark my every move."

They noticed Alu and Mag getting close to them.

Alu's voice cut through the air. "Do you think the barley will jump into your hands?"

A breeze lifted the stalks so they were easier to gather, and Alu sniffed the moving air and smiled. She enjoyed her own sharp humor, and the young women were at ease because the nodules of barley clung together and did not jump into the wind at their touch. Mag and Abun ran to look at the greening trees at the edge of an embankment. Sura fought the desire to grab her son's hand and keep him close. She gathered the barley, her lips drawn in forced concentration. Tehil, not being either boy's mother, stood watching them. At five and three, they wouldn't get lost, but Mag knew how to hide from sight, found only when the shriek of a bruised child pointed to his presence somewhere nearby. His father watched him grow into a willful and arrogant child. There was nothing Manul could do now to interfere. Alu saved the boy's life, and he promised that life to her in return. The only lasting effect of his difficult birth was a thick cough that warned others that he was coming. Protecting the smaller children from his pointed milk teeth and pinching fingers—while not provoking Alu—was a delicate balance to maintain. Didn't the figures she burned in her secret catafalque strongly resemble the recently sick and dying? The thought of that alone sealed one's lips. If someone said it out loud, better to seal your ears. No one confronted her or him. A promise had to be kept, and children had to accept the bumps and bites of life. Alu's boy would one day learn to curb his hunger. Perhaps when something bit him back.

Tehil favored the child of her brother, who emerged into the dangerous world straight and plump and whole, opening his eyes first on her as she severed the knotted cord that connected him to his mother. Tehil said, "You're right, Mother, the barley will not jump into our hands," and in the instant she bent to the ripening grain, both she and Sura heard the unmistakable thump of stone on bone and Abun's sharp cry. They darted to where Mag stood alone, looking down the steep incline. Sura bounded over the edge. Abun lie flat on his back, staring up at the ledge that came up to his mother's shoulder, the breath knocked out of him, his face turning a livid purple. She lifted his head, and he hiccoughed and gulped the air with a ratcheting sound. He howled in pain and pointed toward the ledge where Sura could see Tehil from the knees up and Mag's peering face next to her. She felt the swelling lump on top of Abun's head. Her hand came away covered with blood.

Mag looked down at them with an air of mild interest when Tehil swatted him on the backside and his knees buckled a bit. He kept his balance without changing his expression, and before Tehil could hit him again, Alu came up behind them, grabbed his arm, and pulled him away. Abun cried while Sura worked to stem the blood that spurted from his head. "He hit me with a rock," he wailed as his mother checked for other damage. His elbows were scraped but no broken bones.

Sura didn't ask why Mag hit him. The indulged and cosseted boy had struck again. Two years older than Abun and twice as big, he pulled the younger child's hair and slapped any child who offended his sense of importance. Sura tried hard not to hate him now, but he could have killed her son. The anger she felt was magnified because there was nothing she could do about it. She picked Abun up and carried him back to their camp. The sticky blood flowing from the top of her son's head didn't worry her. Even superficial head wounds bleed for days without killing the wounded. What disturbed her was Mag's delight in hurting others, the way he watched the tears of the defenseless without being moved himself. Tehil's swat didn't even make him blink, so intent was he on watching the effect of solid rock meeting pliant scalp. The last time he used a rock on a child as big as himself, the girl hit him back with enough force to make him rethink the size of his next victim. Alu, who saw the exchange, said to him while she mopped the blood out of Mag's eyes, "Why don't you crack open a rabbit skull? At least we can eat that, and the rabbit won't hit you back."

Sura got back to camp and found Naki sorting scallop shells. A pile already drilled and painted sat on one side of him. "How contented you look," she said. He frowned. If Sura was angry because he looked happy, he would try to look unhappy.

Sura moved the shells aside and laid Abun down next to him. He was sleeping, and his face was streaked with tears, blood, and dirt. Blood seeped from the hole on top of his head, and Sura cleaned him while he whimpered in his sleep.

"Mag did this," she said. "He struck him with a rock and pushed him!"

Naki looked at the wound on top of his son's head.

"Did you see him do this?" he asked.

"I heard it. Tehil saw it. I'm sure Alu saw it, too. And Abun told us that Mag hit him and pushed him so that he fell backward. What are you going to do?"

Naki inspected the boy's scraped arms and legs. "Nothing is broken."

"This time."

"Children fall."

"Yes, children fall," she said, her voice raised in anger, "when some- one hits them on the head with a rock and pushes them off a cliff. And no one does anything about it."

That night, Sura slept with her arms wrapped around Abun. When Naki entered their shelter and tried to lift the child from his mother's arms, she stiffened and held on to him tighter. Naki walked to where his father sat, chewing his toothpick by his fire.

"It's cold," Manul said.

"Manul," a quavering voice called from behind him.

Naki sat down and studied the whistling features of the moon. "Winter is coming."

Manul ignored Fox's voice. "Sometimes the cold is welcome," he said.

CHAPTER TWENTY-FOUR

WOLVES AND MEN

"Bani, tell us about the wolves."

Bani sat at the center of a circle of people from the four clans of the Huul. The old listened and were brought back to the time they sat at the hearths of their parents. The children, the stories new to them, were filled with wonder, anticipation, and a thrill of fear.

"They run fast and far. The wolf searches for us and is afraid of us, too."

"Does he know we don't eat them?"

"It's hard to say what he knows," Bani said. "The wolf watches my face like a child when his mother speaks. I hear his howls and whispers— his voice—raised to signal someone who's far away." Bani sat back on his haunches, stretched his neck, made his mouth into an O, and cried out in a way that all creatures could hear and respond to.

"When you have the same father," a boy said, "you speak the same language. The Mari's father is a lion and they understand its language."

"So they say," Bani said.

"I followed the wolves to the place the NesGras call Wolf's Peak. The gray wolf in front was tall and his face was broad. He climbed higher than the others and rested, where he looked out over a great distance. He could see the path the gazelles take along the river. The big herds cross there, and hunters wait for them to stop and drink. He set his eyes on that spot, and then he looked at me."

"To challenge you?" the boy asked.

"To recognize me and to warn me of his strength," Bani said. "To join him if I wished. I regret that I didn't."

"Was this before or after you fell in the hole?" a little girl asked.

Bani laughed. "After." Bani's misadventure had become a cautionary tale for children to watch where they were going.

"Was he the wolf that showed your brother where to find you?"

"I don't know. He could have been. I didn't get that close. The wolves didn't threaten me, but that doesn't mean they wanted to share their food."

"What did they eat?" the little girl asked.

"I watched them bring down an aurochs—big, but old, and clumsy when she ran. They chased her until she tired. She seemed confused by the snarling circle they formed around her. Maybe she thought of her youth when she could keep up with her brothers and sisters and was too strong, thick-skinned, and sharply horned to be easily brought down. The gray wolf's sharp teeth punctured her artery like two spikes. She surrendered to the bite as if she were falling asleep, dreaming her death, sighing deeply, until the blood in her throat swallowed the sound. The wolf in front, and a female wolf as fast and as big as he was, were the first to eat. The others waited for them to finish, then they carried the meat back down the other side of the mountain."

"To eat later?" the girl asked.

"And to feed their cubs," said Bani.

"Did you see the cubs?" The children's faces were bright with excitement and curiosity.

"I saw them, but not until the next day when I took another path."

"How did they look?"

"Like you," Bani said to a girl, her hair and face grimy from her play harvest of pebbles and chaff and whose yellow eyes looked too big and bright in her narrow Nir face. When the other children turned to look at her, Bani said to all of them, "And like you. But the cubs were not alone. There was a wolf—old, I guess, because her face was white—that stayed behind to watch over them."

"My grandmother stays with me when my mother and father are not there," a very small boy almost cried out, as if the similarity between the young wolf and himself was unbearably familiar and shocking at the same time.

"I found two very small cubs last year, and they were tinier than any of you when you were born. They were sleeping in a hole their parents dug. Their eyes weren't open, and at first, I couldn't tell what kind of animal they were. Instead of long, gray fur, they were black. Their faces were short and wrinkled, and their ears were small and round. I didn't see any adult wolves nearby, and I didn't want to be there when they came back, so I left them. The next day, I brought them mice to eat. I know now that they were too young for anything except mother's milk, but I wanted them"—Bani searched for a word to describe the feeling he had for those blind, mewling creatures—"to be mine."

A man Bani hadn't noticed before spoke. "Yours in what way? Like your child? Like your brother? Like your friend?"

"Yes, all of those things. I think about that day a lot, and I wanted them to be my companions, to join my family—our pack. Do you see what I mean?"

The man shook his head, but Bani couldn't tell if it was because he thought Bani's reaction to the cubs was ridiculous, or because he himself had such feelings without expressing them.

The man asked, "And did they eat the mice?"

"No, the cubs were dead when I got back."

"Who killed them?" a child asked.

"It was cold. A deer may have killed their mother while she was hunting and she couldn't get back to feed them. I don't know. I think if I come across a wolf cub again, I'll wait. If no one comes to tend it, I'll wrap it in my blanket and bring it to my mother's hearth so it won't freeze or go hungry."

By this time, many adults had gathered round to hear about Bani and the wolves. The man who asked about the mice told another story.

"Before my father taught me how to use a spear to kill without wounding, I injured a deer whose antlers were as wide as an oak tree."

"Ooo." They whistled in appreciation of the deer.

"It still ran even though it was hurt, and we followed its bloody path a long way." He paused to give his listeners the weight of time and distance it took to follow the deer.

"We heard a terrible growling from the place the deer ended up, so we crept behind a boulder where we could see and hear but not be seen or heard by whatever was making those noises. To see hunger so fierce, so furious, is like seeing the face of wind snatching your breath. A pack of wolves can smell the red of blood, and they ended the deer's life before it toppled to the ground. The wolves killed without waste, unlike me in my green recklessness.

"Has anyone here not made such a grievous mistake?" He looked around, but no one spoke except a black-and-white bird, urgent in its thousand bird voices. *Tell us more about the wolves.*

"There were so many of them tearing at the ripped and bloody carcass. I still hear them rumbling like thunder, their teeth clamoring against the bones and antlers. We didn't dare move. We were exhausted, and surprised, too, by the raw power of their hunger. How far did the wolves run to catch the deer? We think we passed them earlier, before I wounded the deer, and that they knew what would happen and got to the killing spot first."

A murmur of agreement passed through the growing crowd.

"Then the wolves stopped feeding and looked toward a thicket of trees across from us. Do you know what appeared?"

The children, mouths open, shook their heads *no*.

"An old wolf, his muzzle white and grizzled, lame, hobbling on three, fur-matted legs, made his way to the dismembered but still meaty deer, and the other wolves greeted him, showed him respect . . ."

"Respect," the old people in the back repeated.

". . . and the wolves that had brought the deer down waited for him to finish his meal before they went back to eating."

"I know wolves," Blue said in his coarse voice. Even Bani was surprised to hear Blue speak in the language of the Huul.

He heard people in the crowd say, "The man who fed his arm to a lion."

"The flute player."

"The one brought by the north wind." Not that you could miss him, standing a head taller than most of the other men, his hair as bleached as shore-washed wood, wearing no blanket against the cold, the red, shining stump of his arm raised in a gesture that resided only in his memory. A few did not greet him, holding their mouths and their spears tight and still, finding more evidence of a NesGras peculiarity to dislike—their overabundant and reckless hospitality toward strangers.

Blue swallowed. "My bruzzers," he started.

"*Bruzzers?* What are *bruzzers?*" the crowd murmured.

"His brothers," Bani said, wondering whether the crowd's curiosity or patience would give out first. "He means his people."

Ah. Curiosity temporarily won out.

"Yezz, wolves and bruzzers together."

Now everyone in camp stopped what they were doing to hear about Blue's bruzzers and the wolves. Bani helped him tell this story.

"From my grandfathers' time, wherever they went, they met people with wolf companions. The people have always followed hunting wolves. Then it got so cold in the north that the migrations in spring and fall were broken." Blue chopped his remaining hand in the air to emphasize the disruption. "The berries, nuts, and grass that we eat turned black from the cold. They were slimy and bitter when we tried to melt them by the fire. Lichen and bark hurt our empty stomachs. We ate that, too, when there was nothing else. We moved south, but the longer we traveled, the more my family suffered, until all—except me and the one you called my twin—died. Some stayed and found places that, despite the persistent cold, remained warm enough to survive, sought-after places, which led to more bloodshed and contention. The weakest, who could not fight the cold and the starving animals, along with fighting their stronger brothers, died first. The strongest, the animals that were most like themselves, joined them at their campfires where they learned to share the hunt and enjoy the chase. So much alike."

The people looked in the direction Blue's eyes were focused, watching man and wolf together on an imaginary, frozen plain.

"The young born close to our campfires were truly like our children. We learned from each other. The wolves followed the reindeer, bison, horses, and aurochs, and the people followed the wolves. Who was the first to hunt with the wolf? No one knows, but tracks set in stone deep within the caves there," he said pointing north, "tell us it was long ago."

A young man in the gathering crowd spoke. "Here, by the great sea, the wolves pursue deer and ibex, while we prefer horse and aurochs." Before Blue could continue, a dispute arose about the merits of flesh from the edgy herds of speed-loving horses versus the dangers of mean-tempered aurochs that would form a boulder-strong ring around their young and stamp the life out of any who dared to breach it. The people of the Huul loved to argue, and bluster moved through the crowd like a tangle of dry grass—thorny but weightless.

Blue waited for everyone to remember him before he said, "When the wolf has enough companions, he goes after bigger game."

A tall man who sat down unnoticed among the children said, "Wolves like easy prey—the crippled calf or a graybeard elk. We," he said as he slapped his chest with the flat of his hand as if he represented all people everywhere, "prefer the stag and the stallion."

"No, no," a short NesGras man said. "She defends her cubs from bears. Do you think a bear is easy prey?"

"The female is bigger and faster than the male!" someone said so forcefully that the crowd quieted for a second, then resumed their argument again.

Bani shouted, "Blue's people lived with wolves bigger than the ones that live here."

Blue, Bani realized, couldn't follow the argument in the fast-paced rhythm of the Huul language where no one waited for anyone to finish before shouting out whatever came into their head.

Blue looked at Bani, who nodded for him to continue.

"We took a wolf cub to live with us. She was a traveler that came and went, sleeping at our campfire, hunting with my father, my brother, and me, leaving for a time, returning with gifts. She would lay a rabbit at my father's feet, small animals, a haunch of deer, or a headless vole. She came once with a snout full of porcupine quills, which my father carefully removed. Her tongue was badly cut, so we shared our food with her, small pieces so that she could eat while her wounds healed.

"She was a good companion when she wanted our company. A better hunter in her way than any of us. One spring day, she came back and dug out a shallow den behind a dense bush outside our shelter. My brother carried back a small, black animal. We didn't even know what it was—so round and helpless. My father told us to put him back where we found him and we did. There were four little ones like him, and my brother and I went to see them every day. Their mother let us pick them up. We'd go there even when she was away. One day, before sunrise, we heard a growling, squealing ruckus. A bear held one of the cubs in his mouth. Their mother had left them in the den by themselves while she hunted. Two were already eaten. The mother flung herself from the slope, sliding and lunging at the bear's throat! The bear looked as startled as we were. He dropped the cub, dead already, and roared to show his annoyance at having his meal interrupted. Not until the bear was out of sight did the wolf break her stance. She licked the poor, dead cub, then picked him up and carried him away."

"Where did she take him?"

Blue, seeing that the question came from a small child, answered, "I don't know." The tall man sitting next to him started to tell him, but so many people gave him warning stares that he popped his mouth closed and snorted through his nose.

"There was only one cub left, and he stayed with us long after his mother left and never came back."

CHAPTER TWENTY-FIVE

GOOD-BYE MAG

If an adult was with him, she might have smacked the mushroom out of Mag's mouth, but he was alone when he hunkered down behind the oak so big and old, they called it Tell's grandfather. Mushrooms proliferated under the oaks in the wet spring: giant bracket funguses sprung overnight from the rough trunks; small, orange flattops that looked like they were filled with honey; red, round, sticky balls that appeared as juicy and sweet as berries, yet stung the tongue; nut-like, brown mushrooms, plain as mud, good to eat and easy to dry and stash away for later. He knew all these mushrooms well, and they were not growing under that old oak tree today.

The little girl who didn't move out of his way fast enough finally stopped sobbing, and he felt the need to bite something else just then. The round caps of the mushrooms that were growing near his feet were pale yellow and green, glistening from the recent rain. They each looked remarkably like his boy's penis when it emerged in the mornings and he needed to pee. He touched the mushroom. The shiny cap wasn't smooth as he expected. It was tacky and coated his fingers where he touched it. He licked them. The taste was sweet, leaving only a hint of bitterness at the back of his tongue. He peeled the surface and dropped the skin into his mouth. He knew that only edible mushrooms could be peeled, and he pulled a handful out of the ground. He studied one, waiting to see if he might suffer some ill effects from the small piece he had already ingested. The mushroom had a cup-like structure at its base, as if it were set in a tiny bowl of water. He separated the cap from the stem and drank the liquid from its dainty receptacle. He ignored the flat, tough gray ones interspersed among the ripe looking and freshly sprung. No need to take them when there were so many plump caps within his reach.

His mouth watered. He swept the litter of leaves aside and plucked more mushrooms. Some mushrooms can kill by just touching them, but these looked so inviting, not like those lurid stools that cropped up from the earth like rotting flesh, or the parched, brown growths barely useful as fuel. These were the shape of quail eggs and smelled of honey, and they tasted like nuts without the hard shells to crack. He ate one, then another, and put the rest in his little sack to eat on the way back.

He wasn't far from Alu's shelter. He could see it from the oak-bowered path he took. He felt tired, although it was midmorning and his stomach ached. Brown liquid poured down his legs before he could clench his bowels. He tried to call out, "Alu," but a great upheaval of bile spewed from his mouth. Instead of the relief that came when you expel what makes you sick, his stomach hurt so much more that he had to lie down. He woke up inside, a fire sizzling near his feet and Alu wiping the sweat from his neck. He could hear drums and a keening wail coming from somewhere nearby.

Mag moved his lips. "Has someone died?"

Alu wrung the cloth and dipped it into the shell that held a pleasant-smelling liquid. Lavender and hyssop, warmed by a cedar fire. Mag took note of what he wore. A new blanket swathed him. Not new, he realized, but the cloth that first caressed him.

"I feel much better now, Mother," he said and slipped into a sleep from which he never woke.

CHAPTER TWENTY-SIX

NIN BREAKS THE PEACE

Bani woke to four Nir men standing over him. One had a broken piece of bone in his hand. He threw it hard, and it bounced off Bani's nose and landed beside his head. Bani sat up, not sure for a moment where he was. Neither Nin, his father, his brother, nor any other NesGras was close by. He was awake all night while the others slept, marking his calendar stick with a crescent, recording the waxing moon, intent on making the pictographs as symmetrical as the fractional moon appeared in the sky. One of the Nir gripped it now as if it were a weapon, a narrow piece of wood as long as his arm. He was little more than a boy of Bani's age. It was the same boy who sat beside him at the great meetings, closely following Tell's instructions, quiet and respectful. Now Bani barely recognized him. The boy grimaced and bared his teeth.

"Are you angry with me?" Bani started to stand, and someone pushed his shoulder down hard from behind. The grimacing boy broke Bani's stick in half over his thigh, then tried to break those pieces, too, grunting with the effort. Another Nir man, whom Bani recognized as Naki's brother Dzo, took the broken sticks from him and smashed one with his hammer, the half that Bani had worked on for many nights. Dzo kicked the smooth, unworked half into the fire, kindling now, worthless.

"Leave here now!"

Bani struggled to his feet. He fought to keep his face from betraying the pounding of his heart. He turned to each of the men who surrounded him, looking for a clue to their sudden hostility. Was this a painful initiation into a cypher he had somehow neglected to unravel? As far as he knew, and he tried hard to know, he had broken no Nir pact. He had breached no Nir taboo. Wasn't the old eagle of the Huul his guide? What had he done to be cast out?

"Why must I leave?"

"You know why." Dzo raked Bani's cheek with a jagged fragment of shattered bone and dropped it at his feet.

Bani touched the wound, stunned by the attack. Through Sura, Dzo was his brother. Why was he treating him like an enemy? His heart stung far worse than the bleeding cut. He picked up the sharp piece they used as a weapon against him and saw the circle of the moon incised into it. Where was the rest of it? Why was it broken?

Bani knew who carved the moon. He had watched the thick, blue veins that turned and twisted just below the skin of Tell's hand release the images into the bone—circles as round as the singing face in the night sky, scored crescents with the sharp symmetry of an aurochs' horns, the parallel symbols on the long bone echoing the moon's transformation night after night, waxing and waning, until the cycle repeated. Neither Bani, nor any of the other young people, possessed that precision yet. Very few would ever possess it.

Bani's impulse was to run and ask Tell to explain what happened. He would know that no NesGras would commit such an act of destruction and disrespect. He did not want to leave. There were stories he hadn't heard yet, skills to learn that his father and brother could not teach him. Since Sura joined the Nir, the home mountains of the NesGras confined him. He longed to be close to the sea and to be near the people who lived on its bounty. The horizon beyond which the sun slipped away belonged to them—and to him when he was among them.

Bani could see his family in the distance. Were they coming toward him or moving away? The Nir men had gone in the opposite direction. He saw people moving in close to where they stood. A few people around the edges of the gathering group turned toward him. Even from this far, Bani saw the fear and disbelief on Naki's face. Bani looked for Sura. She would be a bridge from him to his accusers. She would explain that it was not he who broke the cycle of the moon-carved bone. He didn't break the trust that it would appear and reappear as steadfast behind clouds as it was on clear nights, a circle of smoke in a blue sky before the sun set. *Here I am*, it said to anyone who cared to look up. *Follow me, and I will share my secrets with you.*

Esur, Rosh, Xur, Blue, Mina, and Little Blue were all there, walking fast. All they brought with them to the camp was again on their backs. Bani ran toward them.

"Why do we have to leave?"

"Don't you know why?"

"They showed me Tell's calendar."

"Yes."

"I didn't break it!"

Mina said, "We know."

Bani let the tears fall now, mixing with the blood and dirt on his cheek.

"They broke mine, too," Bani said, showing them a scorched fragment rescued from the fire.

"I didn't finish it," he added.

For the first time, Xur spoke. "We leave now."

"Where's Nin?" Bani asked.

Mina looked away. "He's already left."

Bani opened then closed his mouth. Nin. They knew without saying that it didn't matter whether it was Nin or Bani, or whoever had destroyed that stick. Even if one of them had plunged it through Tell's juiceless heart instead of just smashing it in a fit of jealousy, no NesGras would ever reveal the culprit to a Nir.

Bani thought of his sister. "Where is Sura?"

Mina looked away. "She is with Alu and her sisters."

"What will she do now?"

"What should she do?"

Bani realized that they were already moving away from the sparkling sea, away from the abundance of people and food, away from the tellers of stories and explainers of dreams.

"Bha," Bani said, using the child's word for father, "you said the moon would wax and wane whether we note it or not. You said we were foolish to believe that our marks meant we could control the moon. The injury to Tell's measure will not prevent it from appearing. So why are they so angry with us?"

"They marked your cheek as a warning. You are a NesGras who desired something the Nir possess. They are jealous and see the same in others. To them, you are as guilty as your brother. No more and no less."

"Can Tell create another stick?"

"Of course," Bani answered, more testily than he meant to.

"Can Mina create another Nin?"

Bani thought bitterly that one was too many, but this was not the time to provoke his father. Xur put his arm across Bani's shoulders, then helped him pick up his blanket and tools. Esur was already walking east to where the wind gathered its brutal strength.

Two days later, they saw Nin's low fire burning, a desolate signal to the NesGras that he waited to rejoin them. Bani's cheek burned now, although the blood congealed around the crescent-shaped cut, a reminder of what he lost. Together, they passed a stream that longed to run down to meet the greater waters of the valley, water that was cleaned by the stones that arranged themselves in the downhill flow. The birds silently watched the band move higher to the cold-loving trees that found comfort in jagged edges and perilous steps of ice.

Sura came back from one of the long treks with Alu. Abun was getting heavier to carry on her back, but he always walked in the opposite direction when she set him down, then ran as fast as his fat legs would go. Sura ended up chasing him, expending more energy than if she just set him on her shoulders. When she did, he reached for everything, undid her hair, threw her ornaments into the bushes, lurched backward to grab at birds, threw her off balance, begged to be let down, begged to be picked up, screamed with delight when tickled, and laughed all day and slept all night, warm between his mother and his father. Sura ached now for a night's sleep with Naki and her son close when she saw the angry crowd near Tell's shelter.

Naki turned, and when he saw her, he ran to her.

"What's happened?" Sura asked as he took her arm and moved her toward their shelter. He didn't speak until they were inside.

"Your family is gone. They won't be back."

CHAPTER TWENTY-SEVEN

FIRE

Sura knelt to grip the yellow stalks and strained against the deep roots. They held fast. She straightened slowly to avoid waking the ache that dozed in the small of her back like a mean-tempered beast. She tightened the leather around her waist to bind it in place. Her fingers were stiff with strain and cold. Her hands were etched with a network of lines the color of bark. She rubbed them together. The friction burned but did not warm. She pulled a length of ragged doeskin from her sack and tore it into two strips. She wrapped the strips around her palms and through her fingers. She blew on her fingertips until she felt the blood begin to pulse again. At her back, the sea exhaled a freezing mist. Ahead, the shoulder of the mountain barred the path east. Cold wind rumbled down the mountain's flanks and rasped, *You cannot pass now.* The sun, which shone so brightly when she set out, hid behind clouds that threatened to release an arsenal of ice onto the ground.

She twisted and sat, shrinking into her hood like a turtle into its shell. The rough ground dimpled her knees. Sura tugged at her shift so that less skin was exposed to the sting of the wind. The vegetation she expected to find here was gone: more thorns, less pine, little green. Torn from its roots, the bushes were the color of bleached bones, good only to kindle a fire or to hide behind, barely worth the pain it inflicted on the hands that dared to disturb it.

Sura turned back to the stubborn stalks of grass, twined the fingers of both hands through the sharp blades, and pulled hard.

"Who is stronger, you or I?"

She fell back holding the tufts of grass and dangling roots half as long as she was tall. Immediately, she felt a pang of regret, as she always did when arrogance slipped past her resolve. She pulled more grass from the disturbed soil and huddled against a boulder. She lit a fire, wrapped her heavy sleeping robe under and around her, and began to weave a mat from the longest stalks. She grew dreamy while her fingers moved, knotting and twining the stiff blades. She saw herself as if from the top of the mountain, a dark, solitary bundle close to a circle of light in the vast landscape of gray and cold. She shut her eyes against the wind, and in a state between waking and sleeping, she saw the land as it was in the last days of her childhood, her memory bifurcating her life like a path between mountains.

On the other side of the mountain, Xur pressed his back against the boulder that blocked the entry of the cave and fixed his palms on the rough jamb of the opening. He stiffened his arms to pry the massive stone just enough for him to squeeze inside. He bruised his spine in the struggle for balance on the ice puddle that circled the base of the boulder. He considered just lying on the unsheltered ground until the earth became reasonable again or until he was beyond caring if it did.

The tracks Xur followed were gone, as if the animals had worn down from their flesh and evaporated into the air as they climbed. The trees withered, along with the game they sheltered; where stands of oak once flourished, only scrub remained. Hunger inhabited the Huul like a brutal giant who claimed all life for himself.

Xur's body had lost its robust contours. The muscles in his shoulders, only a few seasons ago packed with well-nourished strength, were taut strips holding his bones together. Still, he struggled until the boulder, tired of his insistent shove, moved enough to allow him to enter. The cave was dry, and Xur, too tired to build a fire, lie down and immediately fell asleep. He dreamed the trees were flush with birds. He heard them call to each other and he understood their song. Their sweet, plump bodies filled his sack, and he anticipated the meal they would make. But when he stopped to look at his cache, the birds had turned to stones. The hunger in his dream was real and hurtful, and he woke up from the pain. He heard the chattering of squirrels as he fell asleep again, and they were food for him without the need to hunt. Their fatty flesh smoked, giving off a smell that was so enticing and so strong, his nostrils ached from the sharp plea- sure of their bouquet. But the sting came from the droppings of the bats that occupied the eaves of the cave, and the sound was their stirring as they exited an unseen chimney for their nocturnal flight.

He was awake in the darkness when he felt something scamper up his leg. He snatched at it and felt the small squeak of a mouse in his palm. He bit off the head, spit it out, and swallowed the body whole. Instead of filling the hollow space in his stomach, the undigested remains imploded in a burst of bile. In the rash impulse to devour the mouse, his stomach was devouring itself. Xur spit out what he had swallowed and brought up again and squeezed his way outside. The cold braced him at first, but in a short time, the wind bit and tore at his flesh. He turned his pelerine so that the fur was next to his skin, and reinforced the lining of his foot coverings with scraps of leather. He wrapped his sleeping robe over layers of flapping hide and set on to climb back over the mountain. He walked a long time on his cold-numbed feet until he spotted a red deer tottering on thin legs. He brought it down, ate a portion only big enough to dull his hunger, took the remaining meat, already frozen, and walked the circular mountain path toward the place his family waited.

The deer he killed would feed them for two days. Nin, grown sturdy and strong, was the best hunter, never hesitating to take aim and never missing the prey. Yet, even he had little success and grew angry as the desperate hunger of the group deepened. Xur's wife, Juul, one of the small, dark people of his mother's Willow kin, possessed of their gentle skills and temperament, now spent the days staring round-eyed into the distance. Her hair, black and lush only a short time before, was now brittle and washed in red dust. After two harsh winters, the swelling in her stomach had neither grown nor diminished, nor did she conceive or bleed. Mina's herbs, when she could find them, were useless. She knew that the girl's barrenness was rooted in the lack of food, and that for Juul, even a small scrape or cut would fester and deplete the little strength she still possessed. Fatal weariness, lying down to rest but never rising, was the predator they feared most. If only they could survive this present cycle of cold, they could build their strength and numbers as they did in greener times.

Mina exhorted the spirits for signs of the direction to follow. Nin spent long days away from camp single-mindedly stalking the retreating game, bitter when he failed, and not content when he succeeded. Xur hoped for nothing, prayed for little, and spent all of his strength in support of the others. Now, as he went up the mountain slope, the acrid odor of burning wood roused him. He saw a black cloud rising from the other side of the mountain and forgot the weakness in his legs as he ran to the summit. He saw the orange flames leap higher than the pines that snapped and groaned in pain. He watched the flames consume the thicket, advancing with implacable greed toward the dry branches of gangling oaks that sheltered his family. Through the haze of smoke and cinders, Xur tried to outrun the spreading ring of flames to get to the heart of the fire, but a wall of heat forced him back. He cried out the names of his family, but the fire's voice roared louder.

He threw down all he carried and charged ahead, but the fire anticipated him, zigzagging in a crazy way, extending like a snake, head meeting tail to form a jagged circle around its prey. Xur choked but ran faster until he burst into the shrinking center.

"Juul. Esur. Mina. Bani." He heard Rosh calling out the names of the family and a child screaming in response. But he could see nothing through the haze.

He heard his own name, a shriek of terror coming from the direction of the camp. He followed Juul's voice until he found them, some blasted unconscious by the heat and smoke. Esur and Blue were east of the camp when the smell of the fire caught them. Now they struggled to pull the others through the narrow clearing. Rosh ran with his small children tucked under his arms. Bani supported Zu and Juul. Nin was missing, but in the billowing smoke, there was no way to search for him. They followed Xur through the only escape in the closing ring of fire. They pushed as far away as they could, struggling through a ditch on the instinct that the fire would not cross this muddy gouge in the earth. They collapsed on the ground, gasping for air aspin with burning cinders. The intense heat met a wall of frigid air, and like wrestlers, they pressed against each other, shoulder to unrelenting shoulder. Two giants—fire and ice—fought to hold their ground, oblivious to the creatures caught between them.

Xur retched soot as thick as sludge. His lungs, like an animal buried in him, clawed through his throat to pull at the air. Then he heard a cry so heart-wrenching that the roar of the fire was overwhelmed. He raised his face from the ground and saw Nin, kneeling by his mother. From the west, four Nir hunters, shouting and gesturing wildly with their arms, ran toward the people sprawled on the ground. He watched Nin rise and draw a spear from the bundle he carried on his back. He saw the hunters but heard no words. Nin pulled his arm back and hurled the spear. The hunters' mouths formed circles of surprise. Xur knew them well: Naki, his brother Dzo, and his cousins Jawan and Zuya. Nin's spear floated in the heat-shimmering air. Xur watched the spear bore through Zuya's throat. Everything else was still. Zuya's body arched backward as the spear lifted and suspended him parallel to the ground, then wafted him gently to the smoldering earth. All at once there was great activity, as if time had waited for Zuya to touch the ground before resuming. Esur grappled with Nin, wrestling his remaining spears away from him. Xur, drifting on a warm blanket of ash, saw and heard no more.

Esur shook Xur awake. He raised his head. Esur stood above him, a silhouette against the morning sun. Xur had not moved since falling. A cold night rain damped the fire and the forest smoked and steamed, still alive with dangerous embers that could reignite in a dry wind. Xur remembered little beyond his first sight of the fire, but when he saw Juul dressing Mina's burns, despair cut his heart. Nin sat with his arms wrapped around his drawn knees, his face buried. Naked in the cold, he did not sob or shiver despite the wind. *What a miserable lot we are*, thought Xur, *weak, burned, starved, and one of us gone mad.* Xur rolled over on his back, and Esur hunched down to speak to him. The skin on Esur's arms, legs, and brows glistened with red blisters. Esur bent close to Xur and said, "The Nir started the fire." Xur rose up on his elbows. "Nin was behind them. They were trying to flush game but the fire spread."

Xur thought of the anger the Nir would turn against the NesGras. After all, the Nir could not control a raging fire any more than the NesGras could control Nin's rage.

"Fire feeds the sweetest grass," said Esur. And this was true. The woodlands could recover in one season, more fruitful than before. That was their hope.

But Xur could only think of what the Nir would do. And Sura among them. *Will we ever see that sweet new grass*, thought Xur as he pulled himself off the ground to gather the charred remains of the game that was flushed from the burning land.

Naki, Jawan, and Dzo entered the camp wearing the news of Zuya's death on their faces. They had buried Zuya halfway between the fire and

their camp, the point of Nin's spear still embedded in his throat. The lithe
Zuya, stiffened by sudden death and dreadful cold, lie beneath a bier of
stones to bind his wretched spirit to his bones. It was left to Naki to tell the
Nir that their son was dead, and by whose hand.

Someone ran to get Tell, and soon the camp filled with all those close
enough and able enough to get there in a day's time. Instead of excitement and anticipation, this gathering hummed with tension and fear.
Instead of games and trade, grievances were brought out and bitter talk
was exchanged. The three men told Tell what happened as the larger group
pressed close to hear them. They told how they set fire to the dry grass
that bordered the old oak forest, and how the fire spread and chased them
from the place they intended to hunt. When they described Nin and the
terrible moment of Zuya's death, Tell lowered his gaze to look at them but
said nothing.

Tell remembered Nin, with his stocky body and big head set low on
his shoulders. He remembered Nin's wounded eyes that bore the look of a
trapped animal—frightened, in pain, and very dangerous.

"Tell," they all cried, "what shall we do?"

Tell listened and lie down on the ground. His eyes, gray and trans-
lucent with age, stared without blinking at the sky. The mountains behind
him mimicked his profile. Zuya, his grandson, was dead, killed by Sura's
kinsman. The weather was colder than ever before in his long memory.
Colder than in his youth. Lichen, the staple of the starving, was scarce,
licked from the discarded bark of dying trees, littering the ground that was
bare of vegetation, ice-rutted and hard. The horse and the elk had fled,
angering the lion and the wolf. The tree line shrank back from the summit
of the mountain, exposing the habitat of the small animals that required the
shelter of the oaks and tall pine. The white flowers that rained from the sky
were infinitesimally small and carved from ice, and the surface they formed
on the ground was far more treacherous than the stones they covered. The

numbers of people diminished as the old died younger and the young just died. Fear thrived in the places left empty in those who survived.

Tell was tired. He could see himself from a place that hovered above his body, and he could see his body through the piles of hides and material that failed to keep him warm. His body was desiccated, a fallen leaf buffeted by the winds of time. He could not find enough moisture within himself to shed a tear. He drank little, but when he did, a lonely, viscous drop of liquid would squeeze from the tip of his penis and fall with a listless *sst* on the ground. His heart hammered dryly in his chest, no longer keeping rhythm when he ran. (When was the last time he ran?) He saw his blood as a purple bruise, a painful layer between his brittle bones and his crumpled skin. Still, the people looked to him and asked, "What shall we do?"

Tell's hovering spirit, searching his own shriveled fig of a face, said, "Yes, Eagle of the Huul, tell them what to do."

"Is he asleep?" a child asked.

"No, no, he's not asleep. He's consulting with the spirits."

"Is a spirit here now?" the child asked.

"Yes, I think so."

"What's the spirit called?"

"Be quiet," the exasperated mother said.

"The spirit of the mountain," another voice answered. "Its name may not be uttered."

"Why?" the child started to ask, but a mother's pinch ended the question with a yelp.

Alu bent over Tell, coming between him and his hovering spirit. She helped him sit. He whispered in her ear and she straightened. She ordered the construction of a spirit dwelling, a loosely twined shelter of willow branches. In the middle of the shelter, a fire burned with wolfbane and pepperbush, nightshade and sandalwood. The smoke thickened with the sweet and heavy smell that was unmistakably the spirit of the mountain. People chanted and slapped their feet on the ground. Skins that bore the marks the spirit had revealed were unfurled and stretched across hollow logs. The sound carried beyond the reach of the camp and stirred the weak, the very young, and the very old.

Tell rose from where he sat, his limbs trembling with the effort. Leaning on Alu's shoulder, he shuffled in time to the cadence of the drums. He abandoned the questioning spirit that lingered within him earlier and gave himself completely over to the quest. *What must the Nir do?* He moved his arms, head, and legs and repeated the sacred name in a voice that rustled like a leaf. The tremors in his limbs subsided. His movements grew bold, and blood flowed again in his veins. Time fell away. The sun set and the sun rose, and still Tell went on. The drummers kept their rhythm, and the chanters called the invocations as their voices grew as thin as water.

Lines of light slashed the darkness. Tell was lighter than the ash that spiraled above the fire. He entered through a slit of light above the summit of the mountain to the air the spirit occupied. The spirit held him as a tender mother caresses her child. Rapture cradled him. He wanted to stay suspended above the ache of life. The answer was pressed to his cheek by lips as quiet as a butterfly. The budding lives, the juice and energy of children, could make the treeless ground fertile.

Tell etched the lines of light in the earth. The people knew the signs. He cried out what the spirit required. They knew what they must do. The blood that stirred in his veins was expelled from his eyes like tears. So great was his disappointment that the great mother no longer held him in her arms, that he fell upon the etched lines in the earth and tried to reenter the world of the spirits once more.

Alu and the small circle of chanters and healers emerged from the shelter. The people of the camp pressed close to them. Sura remained at a distance while she fed her children the last of some dried meat mixed with berries conserved for this time of shortage. They stayed close and kept their fires small against the dwindling supply of wood. She could not hear what Tell said. Sura knew that in the days Tell and the others stayed in the shelter, they had neither eaten nor slept. Their fires burned with smoke that transformed their senses while they whirled to the drums that reverberated without ceasing or varying their rhythm. She knew they clamored to reach the spirit world, which they beseeched to command them. She felt isolated, alien, unable to connect with the people or their infected spirits. Whereas Mina taught her to avoid the evil eminences, Alu strove to collaborate with them to accomplish her will.

For the first time since the news of Zuya's death, quiet fell. Dread gripped Sura in its icy claw. Since leaving her people, the din created by the more numerous Nir never failed to unnerve her. Now the sudden silence drained her reason. She forced herself to look at Tell. *Ochre*, she said to herself. *He has painted himself with ochre.* But she knew it was not ochre. Blood streaked from his nose and ears and ran from his eyes through his white hair. He groveled and shrieked and scratched the ground. Sura held her children against her while her boy's curiosity pulled him toward the center of the camp. The people began to ululate and moan, making fearsome music from their terror. They tightened their circle around Tell, and their litany intensified when they saw the signs he slashed in the cold, hard dirt. She saw Naki, his face wet and wrenched back from his teeth in a mask of agony. She would not go to him, afraid to become a part of the madness that swept the camp. Naki ran to her. She looked into his eyes, red and staring, as if shock had ripped off his lids.

"Naki, what is Tell saying?"

The abrupt flicker of Naki's eyes toward their youngest child told her. No icy wind, no frozen ground ever felt as cold as Sura's fear. She gripped the small, squirming body so tightly that the baby began to wail in protest. Sura stared at Naki, his face covered with rime, a dome of ice that revealed the fire that burned under his skin. He believed that the word carried by Tell was rightful and inevitable, but in Sura's stark look, he read her refusal. *No.*

"Sura, we are hungry. Many children will die for the sake of your own."

"Then they will die. But not mine among them."

"You cannot say that. The spirit of the mountain is like a motherless child. She requires another in order to suckle us again."

"Naki, it is not the way of my people." But as she spoke, the fear dug more deeply into her.

Where could she and her children hide? Flat on your back, regarding the stars, the mountains formed a ring around your vision. They sheltered and surrounded you, and now that they were hungry and stripped of their green blanket, beset by the cold, bereft of the animals they had always shared with the people, who was Sura to stand alone against their immensity?

No, it was not the way of her people to kill, yet Nin had killed Zuya. Neither was it Naki's way to harm another, yet despite the agony it caused him, he could sacrifice his child. Sura's reaction unsettled him further. Tell's word was immutable, like Zuya's death, or the cold that poured out of the sky in winter and as hard as the stone core of the mountain. Yet, Sura was prepared to challenge the spirit that pulled blood from Tell's eyes and supported the sky on its jagged shoulders. Naki heard the tales of cruel times before he was born, how the offering of a child had equalized the unstable forces that rampaged through their universe. The stories made him shudder with excitement, but the reality was different. Fear made him weak and powerless.

"I will take my children away from here!"

"How can you can leave, Sura?"

"I can . . . I will."

"Why?" Naki's eyes filled with tears.

"They can't have my daughter, Naki. Not for their spirits. How can you let them?"

"My mother believes she will bring back the herds. They are our spirits, too, Sura."

"Not mine."

"You frighten me. Aren't you afraid? You and they will be dashed against the rocks for your insolence."

"And the obedient, the passive? Haven't they met the same fate? I am afraid, but the spirits have already eaten their fill. One small morsel will not satisfy them. Look at her. Give her your finger to suck. See how she pulls life into her. See how she follows my lips when I speak. You think she doesn't understand, but she does. She is real, Naki, in my arms. What happened before Alu was born is not real to me."

Sura unswaddled the child's arms. Tears dripped from Naki's cheeks and fell on the child as he leaned over her.

"Tell demands—"

"No!"

"Alu says we must. . . ."

"Alu demands our fear. That is what she lives on. Death has always been around us. A child is born and another dies. If the mother lives, she cries all her life for the lost one. Where is the abundance in that? Does the spirit of the aurochs who kills as often as he is killed demand more? Does the horse wish to die for us? Does he run toward our spears . . . or away?"

"You bring a curse on us, Sura."

"I bring a curse on myself alone, Naki. If I could, I would stay and fight Alu. I would not have her help sacrifice another child in the place of my own. But your people have grown. The band has many fires, many shelters, and needs more food than the earth can provide us. My family is small. Xur would welcome us, Naki. I know he would protect us. The NesGras have challenged the clans of the Huul before."

"You cannot live with your brother's band. It's impossible. They are hungrier than we."

"Naki, I have been with you since I was a girl. We have shared everything. You are a good man and a good companion. But you're wrong. I will go and you will not stop me. I will take our children with me. If we die, then the spirits of the wind are too cruel, but I will not be cruel. I will not let them die by the hand of any man. Or woman."

"You will die, Sura. Our children will die, and it will be on your head. You cannot leave such little ones alone and hunt for food. Where is the season of melting snow? It is colder now than it has ever been. The river is dry, and where a creek ran, there is only ice. Can you weave a net to fish? No. Can you hunt alone? No. We can chase a deer for half a day until it drops in exhaustion. But we are carrying our weapons on our backs, not our children."

"Then come with me."

"You ask me to betray my people."

"We are your people, Naki."

"I die, Sura."

"You will live. I am sure of that. You will wipe your face of tears and go back and tell them what I have done. They will be angry with you and they will wish me dead, and they will find another child to sacrifice. I am very sorry, but they will. And maybe the great herds will return. If they do not, I will be blamed. If they do, they will forget me and praise Tell as if he were the spirit of wind himself."

"I promised to protect you from the night."

Naki bent to touch the sleepy boy and the girl. "Hello, Bha," said the boy without opening his eyes. Naki put his cheek against the soft face of the infant and began to cry again, but he turned and walked back toward the center of camp. Sura stood, watching him. When she could no longer see him, she sat on the ground and pulled her children into herself. She muffled her wretched cries in their softness, but nothing could comfort her. *I should have begged Naki to come with us. Instead, I go alone—a lie of pride.*

She let the children sleep a while longer. She would have to walk for days before reaching her family. If she could not compete with the other predators that needed easy prey as much as she, then they would live on lichens and bark, the bitterest of foods. When the wind froze the ice, she would melt it and boil acorns and seeds and chew them for her children to swallow. She wrapped her leggings tightly around her. She removed a string of painted shells and flung them away. She kept the necklace of wooden beads around her neck. The baby liked to touch it with her small fingers as she nursed, and she needed something of Naki next to her heart.

On her back, she would carry dried meat, tubers, nuts, and grease to soothe their faces against the cold and wind. Her spears were short but her aim was true. In her right hand she held her digging stick, sturdy enough to lean on, sharp enough to defend them, and strong enough to penetrate the hard and rimy earth. She would take what rough vegetation the suffering land proffered and create nourishment for her children from within herself. She promised to spare the young of the creatures of the mountain because now she knew their pain too well.

She picked up the baby and placed her in a bunting against her chest. When she straightened, her burden turned her silhouette into a bear whose cubs cling to her for life. This time, she understood the dangers of facing the night alone. She could read the trail of the stars and knew the landscape by day as well as anyone, Nir or otherwise. She wished that Naki were by her side. She wanted to reach for him but knew if she were closer to him, then she could not stop her hand from touching him. She would find her family and replenish their loss with her strength.

She woke her son, who shuddered and fell back to sleep a few times before Sura got him to stand. He leaned against her legs, sliding down toward sleep again. His little body seemed boneless under its wrapping of soft furs. She gave him some of the dried rabbit and a little water to drink. When the North Star faded, she took his hand, kissed the top of the baby's head, and covered it with a shawl. She took her first steps away from the Nir camp.

Sura followed the trail north, which the hunters used to get into the mountains. It was no use trying to make a false start or cover her tracks. She counted on their endless babble of what to do and when to do it—consulting the stars, the entrails of birds, the pattern of flung stones in the dirt—before they would make a move.

She stopped before dawn in a shallow cave and ate a small portion of roots. She slept as much as she could before the children woke, wanting to be fed. Then she continued the trek through the day. At dusk, she came to the place where Naki, Jawan, and Dzo buried Zuya. She added to the pile of stones that covered his body and crushed nightshade over them to ease his pain. She spoke to his spirit the way she could not speak to Naki. The cold and hunger of the last two years, were they not terrible? Did he feel as she did that Nin was broken by adversity and loss, and if he had kept his wits, he surely would not have acted on his deadly impulse? Did he regret his own careless act with fire? She told him the reasons that brought her here, to a desolate space between two families who had fallen back into an abyss of hate and fear. She huddled close to her sleeping children and fell into the state of wishful dreams that beguile an exhausted and troubled mind.

She dreamt that Zuya knelt on his own grave, his head bowed, his mouth moving in unheard prayers. He walked to her and stoked the low night fire. She wanted to tell him to lie down and rest, but even in a dream, she was too tired to move.

It did not snow. They were not attacked. The animals she saw—a round, furry vole and a few mice that scurried across her path—were not worth chasing. The cold afternoon breeze pushed against the young children. She tried walking while carrying them both, but her left arm tired too quickly. She could not let go of her son's hand or pull him along because he would stumble, and bending over to set him back on his feet was too awkward with the heavy burden she carried.

Sura passed a cave that was narrow and dry. It was a well-used resting place. She deliberately walked to its entrance, then stepped away. She searched for another route above the worn path. She trusted Naki to delay a search if bringing her back was their intention. She climbed a hill so steep that the boy's feet lifted off the ground when she gripped his hand. A ledge jutted above her head. She reached up and felt the verglas, a slick layer of ice. Good. Ice equaled water. The baby squalled when the rhythm of Sura's stride was interrupted. She removed her blanket and unfurled it over the ledge. She untied the bundle and threw it after the blanket. The tools clattered but none fell. She lifted her boy first. "Don't move," she said. She tightened the baby's wrappings and lifted her. "Hold your sister," she said as she pulled herself until her elbows were straining against the edge. The boy reached out to help her. "No," she said, "hold on to the baby." She took a deep breath and edged her foot on the narrowest toehold. She swung one leg up, but not high enough to grab on. Another breath, and she swung harder. This time, her heel caught hold and she heaved herself upward in one strenuous movement. She lie flat on the ledge, trying not to think about getting them all down again in the morning.

Her son pulled on her arm, and this time she let him. She built a small fire, and they ate from the food she carried. There was just enough room to spread the blanket. She sang a song to them that went, "Every night there is a new star." To herself she said, "Mother, what have I done?"

As she fell asleep, she took one last look at their small faces. "Good night, Abun, son of Naki. Good night, granddaughter of. . . ." She stopped before uttering a curse on Alu's name. When the time came for her daughter to speak, Sura would name her Mina as a reminder of the woman who became her mother. *Mina, drive out the name that burns my tongue.* And tears that didn't fall scalded her heart. Exhaustion came to bury her fear, and if she dreamed, she didn't remember it.

CHAPTER TWENTY-EIGHT

BURY MY NAME

Morning came too soon. The baby kicked and waved her arms, twisting one way and then the other, trying to roll over and crawl away as Sura cleaned her. The boy, Abun, had just learned to dress himself, sometimes forgetting an underlayer or asking help to tie the knot that kept his tunic from flying off in the wind. He would lose his hand or foot wraps and look at his bare fingers and toes as if noticing them for the first time. He cried once from the lingering burn of the cold after spending a bright day running up, then sliding down, an ice-slicked pass. Sympathy was not offered as his extremities gradually and painfully thawed.

Sura kicked dirt over the small fire. She bundled the tools and food, not much lighter after a meager meal. Despite her care, their presence disturbed the terrain as much as any large and feckless beast. Their attendant smells and sounds were an invitation to eat, or a warning to avoid being eaten. A hearth offers comfort, keeps the fierce at bay, yet how many hearths take a drowsy fire tender or devour an unwatched child? Fire was flesh roasted in a pit, food for the flame, that little bit of warmth in the dismal, cold, dark night. It was a blind monster that consumed itself. It was all those things and more that she could not bear to think about. *Mina.* Her eyes stung with tears.

How far could Abun walk on his little legs? If Sura had to carry both children, along with what they needed to survive, how long would it take her to reach the NesGras? Was there impacted snow on the pass between two boulders? A late summer hailstorm might come without warning and pelt the exposed traveler until blind and beaten down. Could one day make the terrible difference? In trying to save her baby, was she killing her son and herself, too? Everything she was taught about the inevitability of fate abandoned her. There was more than one trail to follow. Which one was safest? Her pride in her strength battled her fear of faltering. Obstacles lurked on the periphery of her vision, and doubt trembled in her gut.

Sura wanted to bend and rely on her Nir family. She wanted to keep the link into their extended circle. She didn't want to be alone on this ice-slicked pass. She yearned for the way it was when she and Naki first came together, before the desolation arrived, when they lived surrounded by cousins and aunts—people, young and old—secure in their noisy numbers. The NesGras were isolated from the other clans of the Huul and they suffered for it. They refused to bow to the force that demanded to be fed while they starved.

Long ago, Mina said that Tell was like the bear that has the keenest appetite for its own cubs. In the end, hunger decides who lives and who dies. The NesGras are trees that cannot bend in the wind and discard their useless limbs; their trunks shatter and they die where they stand. The Nir outnumbered the Willow, the Wolf Moon, and the NesGras combined. One woman could not stop their resolve or feed the wind its fill.

While her mind raced, Sura's hands completed the preparations to move on. She lowered the bundle to the ground first and then lowered her son over the edge, letting him drop the last few feet to the uneven ground. He tumbled and looked up at his mother as if about to cry, but didn't, and he scrambled to the spot below her down-stretched arms. She compressed her lips and fixed him with a warning stare that said *don't move.*

She lowered the infant, secure in a cord web. The baby strained to move her head, the only part of her not wrapped tightly, to take in this new vertical perspective. The boy spread his arms wide to steady the descending baby and cradle her gently to the ground. Then Sura swung over the ledge and dropped to the ground next to them. "Ready?" she said to the boy.

"Ready," he said, and tried to cross his arms in front of him in a posture of command he had seen the men take. His heavy layer of clothing did not allow him to, so he nodded vigorously instead.

Sura's senses pricked. Perhaps a twig was snapped or the wind skittered some leaves across the ground. She put her children between her body and the rocky wall and drew her spear.

Abun cocked his head from behind Sura. "Bha," he said, and ran in front of her before she could grab him. "I looked for you all night."

His father lifted him. "And I looked for you."

Naki's cold, chapped skin stretched like burnished leather over his cheekbones. How long had it been since he last ate? His sharpened features were so much like Tell's, except he lacked the eagle's white stare. Naki's eyes were deep-set and warm and embraced her face. Sura put down her spear. She was surprised that the blood pumping through her body did not spurt from her fingertips.

"Have you come to take us back, Naki?"

"No, Sura, I leave the Nir behind."

"You can never go back."

"No. Forgive me, Sura."

"I don't blame you, Naki."

"The cries were terrible at Tell's grave."

"He was their father."

"More than a father. The stones piled high over his bones skittered. Possessed by his unhappy spirit, they tried to pull it back to rest with his bones."

"Did you see his spirit, Naki?"

"When the few brave enough to bring the stones back looked around, they found that two were missing."

Sura knew he meant two mourners who were there to watch the stones set were not at the grave when the rest of the Nir wailed, pulled at their hair, and called to Tell to show them what to do. The two mourners who never wailed in sorrow, or beat their own heads to drive out the burrowing sadness, were Alu and Tehil.

"Some," Naki said, "wanted to chase you down and bring you back. They pointed to the galloping rocks to find your path. They let their hearth fires burn out and stumbled and lurched in the ashes so that only their wet eyes carried the light of life. I knew your path better than the wind. I traveled to the higher mountains of the north, to your mother and father.

"When Alu walked up to the grave, the Nir made way for her. The rocks—I swear this is true, Sura—settled back on Tell's grave, waiting as we all were for a sign."

"What sign did Alu bring?" Sura pressed Naki more, wanting to hear the worst, seeing the heartbreak in his face. "Did Alu come alone, Naki?"

"Alu said Tell's daughter is there. She pointed to the lair of the wind, to Wolf's Peak. At first, the people thought she was talking about herself. About the past. Others thought she was talking about the child." He looked at his sleeping daughter. "Somehow, without them doing more than making a great noise, Alu had followed Tell's terrible vision."

Sura put her hand over Naki's. "Where was Tehil?"

"It was she who climbed. Alu held Tehil's clothes and spread them on the ground. They pushed close to see. Some swore they saw blood. Everyone saw something different. I saw Tehil's cape that her poor, dead lover gave her, the beads that I made for her before I ever met you, Sura, and her foot wrappers lined with rabbit because she said her feet were always cold."

Naki's voice came from high in his throat, keening and trapped. "Alu said that Tehil would embrace the wind, would satisfy its hunger by meeting it where it lives. . . ."

"Naki, we'll go and find her." She slipped on the ice that slicked the ground where they stood and would have fallen, except she gripped Naki's hard arm.

"She wore only her shift. Wolf's Peak is too cold for living wolves' winter fur. Bears sleep, hiding from the wind. Birds are gone. There is only white sky hiding a starving spirit."

"Tehil is strong. She could be in a cave, waiting for us to bring her a blanket."

"She's not waiting, Sura. Tehil chose to take our daughter's place. She climbed, she wasn't carried like a soft-boned baby, unaware of danger. She didn't cry out loud or tell anyone other than Alu what she was going to do. She didn't feign bravery in the hope that someone would stop her before she came to harm. Should we live through winter, we will thank her. And thank the wind, too, for sparing us this time."

Sura let go of Naki's arm and covered her face. "She said I was selfish, and that my selfishness was a good thing. I wish she was selfish and that she was here with us instead of freezing and alone."

"Tehil!" Abun ran and called out her name. "Tehil!"

They caught up with him and wrapped him in their arms. The baby, jarred by the sudden movement, cried and looked around her, frightened, until she saw her mother and father, their arms entwined around her and her brother, who struggled to break free.

"Shh, shh." They tried to comfort him. "Listen."

Together, Naki and Sura said, "The wind is calling. Do you hear it?"

"It said *whrrr*," Abun said, blowing hard through his lips.

"Yes."

"Tehil says not to worry."

"I don't see her," he said, turning to the high point behind them.

"She's there, Abun. She says she went there to keep you and your sister safe."

"How?"

"She is whispering in the mother bear's ear. She tells her to care for you as she cares for her cubs. When the fledglings appear in the spring, she will find you. But you have to pay close attention. She will leave you signs, and we'll help you see them. Can you do that, Abun?"

He nodded, glancing around for a sign that Tehil might already have left for him to see.

"You said she was freezing and alone. And dead."

Sura and Naki looked at each other. They had forgotten Abun heard and understood.

"And you're crying. You tell me not to cry, and you cry all the time."

"We're not crying," Sura said, ashamed to be lying to her son. "We're worried that Tehil might be cold because she forgot her clothing."

Abun looked skeptical and Sura's smile trembled. The lie comforted her, too. Tehil was dead, but somehow she wasn't. In the vast, distant, eternal, unknown cold, there must be room for hope.

That night, one day closer to the NesGras, Naki stayed beside them. She looked at his sleeping face, his mouth relaxed, his breath whistling through the space between his front teeth, his wide cheekbones and forehead smooth, the deep line cut by sorrow between his eyes invisible now. Sura drew her robe over them, and they were comforted. Her heart lay open, warmed and sweetened like a chestnut split in the fire. She was clotted with tears of relief. She only had to look at the path in front of her where other eyes kept watch. The inverted sky was tangled with stars over the sleeping mountains. The threatening blanket of snow that hung over them was thrown off. She would miss Tehil forever, for now she had made them safe, and her gratitude ameliorated the sorrow and fear.

"Do not lift me now," she whispered, and pressed her palms against the bare earth, greedy for life. "I do not want to leave you."

Beyond the mountain that rose across the valley, a band of NesGras climbs to where they will wait for her. Five men, two women, and two children. Focus and you can recognize them: Esur's spine is twisted by arthritis, but his legs carry him and his arms are still powerful. His brother Rosh strides beside him, ready to support him if he falters. Xur, despite his limp, leads. He is sure of the meeting place that Sura keeps in her mind, a place of many caves where old NesGras bones will welcome them and point their way.

Even though the ice is thick, they remain sure-footed and support each other in the face of the wind that pushes against them from the frigid north. The mountain wears more snow, and the eternal sea, which they will glimpse when they get to higher ground, is gray and brackish. They will wait for their daughter there, then they will leave the Huul together and follow the mountains that curve like the crescent moon around the vast, enduring sea.

They are the NesGras, and they will bury their names in the ground and move on.

ABOUT THE AUTHOR

Pat Kranish loves living in the past and sets much of her fiction in the Ice Age—even though she hates being cold and left New York eleven years ago to live in Las Vegas.

"New Life", "The Bear", and "The Time Before Memory", stories excerpted from *Wind—A Novel of the Ice Age*, have been published and enjoyed (maybe wept over too) by readers who share her appetite to go back in time and explore the lives of the ancient people who lived in the mountains that ring the Mediterranean Sea.

Nevada is the setting for three more published stories, one set in the 1970s and a bit autobiographical, and two more from the time when the last of the big toothed cats, and beavers as big as cave bears, roamed the wet and cold landscape.

Pat lives with her husband Mike, and not too far from her three grown children, who wonder what she sees in the etched rocks and faint footprints left by people who lived here so long ago. Look for her upcoming newsletter, *Dispatches from the Ice Age*, for the latest news from the earliest times.